The Ultimate Computing Glossary for Advanced level

Ray Bradley

Published in 2004 by:
Nelson Thornes Ltd
Delta Place
27 Bath Road
CHELTENHAM
GL53 7TH
United Kingdom

04 05 06 07 08 / 10 9 8 7 6 5 4 3 2 1

A catalogue record for this book is available from the British Library

ISBN 0 7487 9377 1

Page make-up by Mathematical Composition Setters Ltd

Printed and bound in Great Britain by Scotprint

Introduction

Welcome to a unique glossary! It is intended for students who are undertaking AS and A2 level computing for the AQA examination board, but should be extremely useful to students on other 'Advanced level' or equivalent courses.

This glossary can easily be used as a stand-alone **reference** and **revision book**, but has been designed as a companion to accompany the main resources (shown in the bulleted list) for AS and A2 Computing. *The main texts fully integrate with this glossary by highlighting entries as they occur in the text.*

- Understanding AS level Computing for AQA
- Electronic Resources for AS level Computing for AQA
- Understanding A2 level Computing for AQA
- Electronic Resources for A2 level Computing for AQA

Using the glossary

This glossary has been **colour coded** to enable students of AS Computing to easily ignore concepts needed for A2 only. The **AS entries are shown in red**, and the **A2 entries are shown in blue**. Obviously A2 students will need to know all of these definitions, as many of the AS concepts are needed for A2, which contains a larger number of synoptic elements compared with the AS course. Many concepts in computing also have multiple meanings, or can be taken to higher levels; much care has been taken to ensure that only the information that you need know is included here. However, a few entries not specifically required by the board are included where this helps to explain material that is required.

Unlike other glossaries, all definitions contained within this one are appropriate to students of advanced level standard. You are not presented with hundreds of concepts that you don't need to know. Many of the definitions **flag common mistakes** that are made by students at 'AS' and 'A2' level. A couple of examples of this occur with the terms 'backup' and 'compiler', and these entries are shown below to illustrate how this is achieved.

Backup A backup is a copy of computer **data** *to be used in the event of an emergency* like a **hard disk** crash, a user inadvertently deleting a **file** or corrupting the data. A backup copy may be created on **tape** or another **disk**. Do *not* confuse this with the term **archive**.

Compiler **Software** that converts a **high-level language** into **machine code**. It does this by creating the **object code** that is to be run on the target machine. If any errors are found during the compilation process, then the **source code** will have to be recompiled. A **compiler** should be compared with an **interpreter**. Do *not* confuse this software with an **assembler**.

The **bold entries** show other terms, which *may also be looked up in this glossary*, and are therefore very useful for cross-reference purposes.

Object-oriented analysis

A large number of new entries concentrate on **object-oriented analysis**, defining terms like '**class diagrams**', '**associations**', '**dependencies**', '**operations**' and '**aggregation diagrams**', for example. *These terms are needed for the module* 6 **A2 project** *from the year 2006 onwards* if you choose to solve a problem by using an **object-oriented programming language** like **Java**, **C++** or **Visual Basic.NET**.

Using the glossary for revision purposes

Some glossaries give very terse definitions with little or no further explanation, (as shown by the first entry in the example below) but *this glossary explains each term more fully*, as shown by the second entry. As you can see, our definitions are more user friendly, highlight other entries in the glossary which help with the explanation, give simple examples and some helpful advice too.

> **Fact** An unconditional truth consisting of a predicate and zero or more arguments.
>
> **Fact** This is a term used in **logic programming**. It helps the programmer to express *something that is unconditionally true*. A fact consists of a **predicate** and a number of **arguments** (which could be zero). Examples of facts from the **Prolog** language are 'female(julie).', which expresses the fact that Julie is a female (one argument) or 'father(james, ray).' which expresses the fact that James is the father of Ray (two arguments). An example of a fact with zero arguments is 'hot.' Each fact in Prolog must be terminated with a full stop, and the programmer must make sure that the order in which the **arguments** occur is consistent.

Hundreds of examples appropriate to the AQA board have been included, and this means that you learn these definitions as they are used in your AS and A2 courses.

Finally, *because* most definitions contain appropriate examples, this book is very useful indeed for **revision** purposes. Students at the author's school, each armed with a copy of this glossary, split up into opposing teams and quiz each other at random. The team answering the question must have their glossaries closed, and the person who is asking the question can choose a term at random. This works well during both years of the course because the entries are colour coded for each year.

Ray Bradley

A2 project An *extended piece of coursework* undertaken by students during the second year of their course. A **database** or programming project fits the **mark scheme** best, but a **web site** may be undertaken if it has a significant programming element, such as linking a **form** to a database using **active server pages**, for example.

Absolute address The **address** of an *absolute position in* **main memory**, like memory location 4F36Hex, for example. It is bad practice to use absolute addressing when writing **assembly language** programs because it limits the places in memory where code may be placed. A relative address is much more versatile.

Absolute path name This type of path refers to the actual location of a particular resource. Typically this might refer to a part of a particular hard drive on a particular computer, or a particular server-based resource on the **Internet**. This should be compared with the term **relative path name**.

Abstract data type Abstract data types allow the programmer, via the **syntax** of the language, to implement **data structures** such as **stacks** and **trees**, using a suitable degree of *abstraction* (i.e. removed from how it is actually implemented inside the computer). Thus, the programmer can work on complex data structures in blissful ignorance of the 'nuts and bolts' needed to carry out these processes in practice. This type of abstraction is particularly important when dealing with **object-oriented programming**.

Acceptance testing This is a phase of the implementation of a new system during which *the company who produced the system hands over complete control to the customer.* Once the analysts, programmers and engineers have left the customer's site, it may still be necessary to fix **bugs** in the system, and this would be carried out as **system maintenance**.

Access rights On professional **operating systems** it is possible to set *security permissions* such that a limited number of people have access to certain **files**. This is how network **file servers** are organised. For example, people can't access work belonging to others, or they may share access to public files. A variety of different security settings exist, like 'Full Control', 'Modify', 'Read & Execute', 'Read' and 'Write'. Using these settings in combination with **passwords**, **user names** and **groups** gives a very sophisticated set of *access rights*, enabling large and complex networks to be managed very effectively.

Accumulator A **register** inside the **ALU** which is used to *accumulate* results.

Acrobat See **Portable Document Format**.

Acronym A 'word' made up from the beginnings of other words. E.g. **MIME** is Multipurpose Internet Mail Extensions and **BASIC**, the **high-level language**, stands for Beginner's All-purpose Symbolic Instruction Code.

Active server page An active server page enables you to create a *dynamic* **HTML** page (i.e. *a page in which interaction between the user and the* **file server** *may take place*). It thus provides similar functionality to that provided by **CGI scripts**, for example. Active server pages are used on Microsoft's Internet Information Server, a web server which may be hosted either on a **LAN** or a **WAN**. Active server pages are often used to link **forms** filled in by the user to a **database** resident on a **web server**.

Actuators See **transducers**.

ADC See **analogue to digital converter**.

Additive colour system The **RGB** system used inside computer **monitors** to build up colours by adding light. Red + Green + Blue makes pure white light. Any colour that a monitor can display is capable of being represented with varying combinations of these red, green and blue colour components. In practice *three electron guns* are used inside a CRT monitor, and these make Red, Green and Blue phosphors glow on the screen. These tiny phosphor dots are very close together, and thus give the illusion of other colours being produced. This should be compared with **CMYK** or **subtractive primary colours**.

Address A number used to *uniquely identify* a location in **main memory** or of some **peripheral** device, or some location inside a peripheral device, for example memory location 2,345,754 in **RAM**. An address is also used in the context of an **IP address** for a **machine** on a **network**.

Address bus A *parallel* group of wires that carries **data** representing the **addresses** of **memory** locations within the computer, or the addresses of **peripheral** devices such as **graphics cards**, **network cards** or **disks**.

Address mask See **subnet mask**.

Addressing modes Addressing modes are used in **assembly language** programming to *describe the different ways in which a microprocessor is allowed to calculate an address.* As an example, if only a single **byte** is available, then 255 different memory locations may be addressed or 256 bytes if you include zero. Also see **register addressing**, **immediate addressing**, **direct addressing**, **indirect addressing**, **indexed addressing** and **base index addressing** as examples.

ADSL See **Asymmetric Digital Subscriber Line.**

ADSL modem A special type of **modem** required to connect an **ADSL** line to a computer.

Agent An agent is software, typically set *up to perform some specialist search and information gathering, or, more powerfully, to undertake autonomous activities, working with other agents to gather and process information.* At a simple level a **shopping bot** might find the 'best' bargains on the Internet, or a different type of agent might correlate searches between different **search engines** like the 'Copernic' system, for example. At the other extreme an agent may be programmed to carry out a set of rules, like 'correlating available beds in hospitals', for example. These agents have the ability to learn, to make their own decisions and to interact with other systems and cooperate with other agents. An agent is also known as a **bot** or an **autonomous intelligent bot**.

Aggregate function These are functions like AVG(), MAX() and MIN(), available in **SQL**, *to perform functions on selected data held in a* **relational database**.

Aggregation This is a term used in **object-oriented analysis**. It means *building up an* **object** *from one or more objects that already exist.* It therefore represents an 'is a part of' relationship. Aggregation may be shown diagrammatically by using an **aggregation diagram**. See also **object-oriented analysis** and **object analysis diagram**.

Aggregation diagram This diagram is useful for helping to undertake an **object-oriented analysis** *before any* **object-oriented programs** are written. *An aggregation diagram shows building up a new* **object** (usually shown in a square box) *from existing objects* (also shown in a square box). *The names of the objects are written in each of the boxes, and a solid connecting line between the boxes has a diamond shape as it goes into the box, which represents the new object.* As an example, the academic departments in a school (e.g. Maths, English etc.) could be used to build up an object called 'School', because the academic departments *are part of* the school. The diamond shape mentioned above would be drawn on entry to the box representing the 'School' object, because many departments (objects) make up the school. If you are undertaking an A2 project involving an object-oriented language like **C++, Java** or **Visual Basic.NET**, then you should have this type of diagram in the **analysis** section of your module 6 project. See also **object-oriented analysis** and **object analysis diagram**.

AI See **Artificial Intelligence.**

Algorithm A *sequence of instructions* (like a computer program, diagram or cookery recipe) to solve a particular problem in a *finite* amount of time. An algorithm will usually have some input data, like an unsorted list, for example, and some output data, like a sorted list. An algorithm thus works on the input data to produce the appropriate output data. Algorithms are ideal for modern computers, which work through programs in the same sequential manner. You should appreciate that some problems are not computable. I.e. it is sometimes *impossible* to find an algorithmic solution to a problem, no matter how much time is spent trying to solve it, or how much computing power is available to work on the problem. Algorithms are ideal for expressing problems when using the **imperative programming paradigm**.

Alpha testing This is the stage that usually follows **unit testing** and **integration testing**. *Selected customers might be invited to the software vendor's site to help check that a system is working properly.*

Alphabetical pointer The name given to a **pointer** (number or **vector**) *which points to the next item of an alphabetically ordered set of data.* Such pointers are useful for helping to implement **linked list data structures**.

Alternate key This is a term applied to any **candidate key** field which is *not* used as the **primary key**. It is possible for a **table** to have more than one **field** that could be used as an alternative for the primary key, and this would be an example of a candidate key.

ALU This is the Arithmetic Logic Unit. It is the part of a **microprocessor** used to work out **arithmetical operations** and **logical operations**. One of the most important **registers** associated with the ALU is the **accumulator**.

American Standard Code for Information Interchange This is an agreed set of codes consisting of just 7 **binary digits** which is used to transfer information like 'letters', 'numbers', 'punctuation' and special **control codes** between computers that support this standard (virtually all do). Without agreed codes it would be impossible to communicate effectively. You should contrast **ASCII** with **Extended ASCII**, **Unicode** and **EBCDIC**.

Analogue signal A signal that can *vary continuously* between some maximum and minimum. Many naturally occurring signals, like 'sound' and 'temperature', for example, are analogue in nature. These signals must be converted into **digital signals** *before* they can be processed by a modern computer.

Analogue to digital converter This is an electronic circuit which converts **analogue signals** into **digital signals**, which would then be ready to be processed by a **computer**. A **DAC** would be needed to convert the signals back again into analogue form, ready to be transmitted over an analogue transmission system like a basic telephone line, for example.

Analysis (1) This is the stage of the **system life cycle** which happens after a **feasibility study** has been carried out. It is a *detailed analysis of the problem*, which may include, amongst other things, using **hierarchical diagrams**, splitting up the problem into subsystems by suitable modularisation. As details about the inputs and outputs are required, then the construction of **data flow diagrams** and how you are going to model the data (e.g. **ER diagrams** if a database is being modelled) might be included. Suitable **data**

dictionaries may be used, together with suitable **tables**, which may need to be **normalised**. It is also usual to quote the likely **software** and **hardware** that might be required.

Analysis (2) This is the section of your **A2 project** where you analyse a problem and agree what needs to be done with your **client** by producing a list of **objectives** or producing a project specification.

AND (1) This is a **logical operation** which can be used to combine **logical expressions**. For example, the **program statement** 'If x = 3 AND y = 2 THEN Z = 4' could be used to put the value of Z = 4, only if x has a value of 3 AND y has a value of 2. *If both of these conditions are not met then the value of Z does not get altered.* Here the program statement contains logical expressions combined with the logical operation 'AND'.

AND (2) A **logical operation** usually performed on pairs of **binary digits** held inside **registers**. *The output of an 'AND' operation is a '1' only if all the inputs are '1'.* Two registers can be used to perform the 'AND' operation, and each bit in one register is usually ANDed with the equivalent bit in the other register, with the answer (the bit pattern obeying the rules outlined here) stored in the **accumulator**. This operation is usually available in both **high-level languages** and **low-level languages**.

Animation The perception of motion created by playing a sequence of images fast enough to fool the human eye into thinking that the images are moving. About 20 images displayed each second is sufficient to do this.

Annotated listing (1) This is useful for your **AS project**, especially if you have used a **high-level language** solution. It is a listing of any code that you have produced together with **comments** which aid readability.

Annotated listing (2) This is an essential part of the technical solution to your **A2 project** in which any **program code** or **macro** code is listed together with an appropriate number of **comments**. It is helpful if the program code has good **program structure**, is modularised, properly indented and easy to follow.

Anti-virus software This is **software** which is designed to *protect against infection* by known **viruses**, and to remove known viruses from the system. All anti-virus software will detect known viruses, and most will also look for common methods of infection and **flag** suspicious programs that might cause problems. It does this by detecting processes typically carried out by a computer **virus**, like storing illegal data in the boot sector of a **disk**, for example. The system can usually be set up by the user to automatically delete infected file(s), to give the option of deleting the infected file(s), or to put infected file(s) in a quarantine area on the disk.

Applet This is a small application which is temporarily loaded into a larger application program and then executed to provide extra functionality. A typical example would be **Java applet**, but applets are also used in **application software** like Microsoft's word processor to provide extra functionality like 'the ability to edit sophisticated mathematical equations', for example.

Application layer This is *layer seven* of the **ISO OSI model**. It is the top layer of the model and *has the job of servicing the communications requirements of applications* like **e-mail**, helping to save files from a **word processor** to the **network file server**, or handling network printing, for example. It also provides for **password** checking. It is this final layer that links the network to the **application software** being used by the user.

Application package See **application software**.

Application software The **software** that is *designed to carry out specific tasks for the users of the computer system, rather than the tasks needed by the computer system itself.* Application software is sometimes classified into **general purpose application software** (e.g. word processors and spreadsheets etc. designed to be used by all) or **special purpose application software**, like a 3D modelling and rendering package used in a film studio. It is common to bundle several packages like word processors and spreadsheets etc. together to form an **application suite**. Software like 'computer programming languages' and other specialist programs used by **application programmers** and system programmers do *not* form part of application software. **Application software** should be contrasted with **system software**. See also **integrated package**.

Application suite A collection of programs designed to *work together* to perform a useful function. Good examples are the 'Office Suites' which usually consist of a **word processor**, **spreadsheet**, **database**, **presentation package**, a **Personal Information Manager** and **e-mail** facilities. Some examples of application suites are 'Microsoft Office' and 'Lotus SmartSuite'.

Applications See **application software** and **application suite**.

Applications programmer A *person* who writes **application software**.

Appraisal This is the final part of your **A2 project** where you *critically evaluate how your project works.* It is usual to compare what actually happens with what was intended to happen in the list of **objectives** produced when the problem was looked at during the **analysis** phase. It is essential to get some critical feedback from your **client** at this stage.

Archive This is *little used data taken* **off line**. If it is needed at some later time, it's usually put back **on line** by retrieving it from an archive **disk** or **tape**. An archive is *not* the same as a **backup**, which is used in the event of an emergency for data recovery purposes.

Archiving This is the act of producing an **archive**.

Arguments This is similar to the term **parameter**, which describes **variables** or **constants** that are passed over to a **function** or a **procedure**. As an example, for the function X = SQR(4), which is a **program statement** to evaluate the 'square root' function, the number 4 would be the argument. As another example, in a **Prolog** program, mother(jane, mary) would be a **fact** that Jane is the mother of Mary. Here Jane and Mary are the arguments.

Arithmetic overflow This means that an error has occurred producing a *number that is too big to be held in the available* **register**. As an example, if just 8 **bits** are available to store positive **integer binary numbers**, then arithmetic overflow would occur if numbers are greater than 255, because this is too big for the 8-bit register to hold.

Arithmetic underflow This means that an error has occurred producing *a number that is too small to be held in the available* **register**. As an example, if just 4 **bits** are available to store a **fractional binary number**, and **two's complement** notation is used, then arithmetic underflow would occur if the number is < 1/16, because this is too small for the 4-bit register to hold. (1/16 would the smallest number that can be held by the 4-bit fractional register.)

Arithmetical operations Operations like 'Add', 'Subtract' and 'Multiply' carried out at **machine code** level inside a **microprocessor**.

Arithmetical shift This is a term normally associated with **assembly language**. A **shift** operation *in which the sign of the number contained inside the register is preserved* is called an arithmetical shift. Compare this with a **logical shift** operation.

Array A multi-dimensional **data type** (could also be a single dimension) where the individual elements of the array (all elements must be of the same data type, i.e. they should be **homogeneous data types**) are accessed by using a suitable **subscripted variable**. A
typical subscripted variable might be something like A(2,4) which would reference the value on the 2nd row and 4th column in a two-dimensional array called A.

Art package See **paint package**.

Artificial Intelligence This is **software** on a computer carrying out tasks that, if carried out by people, would be regarded as intelligent. Typical tasks might be **expert systems**, 'voice recognition', 'language translation', 'context-sensitive help' and the 'ability to adapt to new situations by learning from experience'. There are numerous arguments about whether computers will ever be able to exhibit intelligence. Some scientists believe it to be impossible, but others (the strong AI community) feel that it's just a matter of time.

AS project Your AS module 3 project is *a set exercise designed by the examination board*. The solution to this project is provided by using a **database** or a **high-level language** or a *combination of both*.

ASCII See the **American Standard Code for Information Interchange**.

ASCII file See **text file**.

Assemble This is a term normally associated with **assembly language**. It is the *actual process of converting the* **source code** *into* **object code**, and *linking* with any **libraries** or **macros** that may be needed to assemble the program.

Assembler **Software** that *translates* **assembly language** into **machine code**. Do *not* confuse this term with a **compiler** or an **interpreter**.

Assembly language A representation of **machine code** instructions using **mnemonics**. It is appropriate to program in assembly language when *speed of execution* is of the essence or a particular feature is *not* available in a **high-level language**. See also **second-generation language**.

Assignment In a **programming language**, assignment means 'working out the value of the right-hand-side of an assignment statement and putting it equal to the value of the variable on the left-hand-side'. Because assignment is *not* the same as in an algebraic equation, symbols like ':=' are sometimes used in preference to the '=' sign. This gets over misunderstandings with assignment statements like 'x = x + 1', which would indeed be *mathematical nonsense*. In computing it means add one to the current value of x and put it equal to the new value of x.

Association This is a term used in **object-oriented analysis**, and describes one sort of **relationship**. *An association is a connection between two* **classes** *or* **objects**. For example, one class may interact with another class or depend on another class; it is therefore *associated* with the other class. *An* **association diagram** *can be used to visualise this interaction or dependency*.

Association diagram This type of diagram is useful for helping to undertake an **object-oriented analysis** *before* any **object-oriented programs** are written. An association diagram consists of square boxes representing each of the **classes**, or each of the **objects**, into which the class (or object) names are written. *If we are dealing with classes then each box has three compartments, with the name written in the top compartment. If we are dealing with objects, then a simple square box is used with the name of the object written inside*. A solid line joins the two boxes, and an arrow shows the direction/s of the association. As an example, for two classes called 'employee' and 'employer', the association might be 'works for' with the arrow pointing from the employee to the employer. If you are undertaking an A2 project involving an object-oriented language like **C++**, **Java** or **Visual Basic.NET**, then you should have this type of diagram in the **analysis** section of your module 6 project. See also **association**, **object-oriented analysis** and **object analysis diagrams**.

Asymmetric Digital Subscriber Line A term used to describe the system where the received data (at the user's end) is obtained at a greater rate compared to the transmission of data (from the user's end to the **ISP**). It is thus ideal for most **Internet** connections. Although an ADSL connection may be 'permanently connected', or 'connected for long periods of time', it is still regarded as a **dial up connection** *because you have to dial up your ISP* making use of a modem. To get a real *permanent* connection you need to make use of a **leased line**.

Asynchronous This means that two events are *not* synchronised in time. A good example of asynchronous events happens when **asynchronous data transmission** is used. This should be compared with **synchronous** events, which usually happen under the control of an electronic **clock** inside the computer.

Asynchronous data transmission This is the transmission of data where the transmitting and receiving ends are *not* synchronised with each other. Most long-distance (greater than a few metres!) communications are **asynchronous**. Without some form of 'synchronisation', it would not be possible to correctly interpret the data being received, and this is often achieved by sending the data at a defined rate (bits/sec), and then using **start bits** and **stop bits** for synchronisation purposes.

Asynchronous transmission mode This is a *popular networking system for* **WANs** *and some* **LANs**. Unlike **Ethernet**, **ATM** is *designed with simultaneous transmission of 'computer data', 'real time video', 'real time audio' and 'voice' in mind.* This technology utilises a continuous stream of cells, some of them empty. In this way telecommunications companies can provide a **guaranteed bandwidth** for systems like video and voice, where interruption of the signal would not be acceptable. Switches are available to convert between ATM and Ethernet. **Wideband ATM** is now available, giving increased speed compared to ordinary ATM.

ATM See **Asynchronous transmission mode**.

Attachment This is *a file, in any form, attached to an e-mail* such that the file may be processed or opened assuming that the recipient has the appropriate **application software**. Typically an attachment might be a word processor document, picture or video clip, for example.

Attributes This is the term used to describe the '**fields**' or columns in a **relational database**. Several attributes make up a **record**.

Authoring package A **software package** specifically developed to enable authors to construct effective **Computer Based Training** (**CBT**) or **Computer Aided Learning** (**CAL**) packages. Sophisticated authoring packages allow for full control of multimedia resources, and allow for a variety of different paths through the material based on the analysis of a student's performance.

Autonomous intelligent bots These are **agents** that, *once programmed, can perform their tasks unaided*. They can gather and correlate information and a large variety of **bots** are becoming very sophisticated indeed. They are set up to gather information on a variety of specialist subjects from 'artificial intelligence' through to 'distributed problem solving'.

Backbone In **network topology**, this is the *main communications highway* that is used to connect different networks together. A typical example would be a high **bandwidth fibre-optic** link that links different networks in an organisation like a school or college. **Managed hubs** and **routers** are usually used to make sure that local data does not get put on the backbone unnecessarily, or this may slow down the effective bandwidth.

Backup A backup is a copy of computer **data** *to be used in the event of an emergency* like a **hard disk** crash, a user inadvertently deleting a **file** or corrupting the data. A backup copy may be created on **tape** or another **disk**. Do *not* confuse this with the term **archive**. Backups should be made at regular, and preferably frequent, intervals.

Backus Codd Normal Form This is one of the rules carried out to ensure errors are minimised when designing a **relational database**. This rule states that *a relation is in* **BCNF** *if every* **determinant** *is a* **candidate key**. You should remember that data must already be in **third normal form** before attempting to put it into BCNF. See also **first normal form**, **second normal form** and **third normal form**.

Bandwidth For any communication link (radio, network, telephone etc.) the bandwidth is *the difference between the highest and lowest frequencies that can be transmitted* (i.e. the width of the band of frequencies being used). However, in computing this term is commonly used to mean *the number of* **bits** *that can be transmitted each second*. (You will, for example, hear people say 'What Internet bandwidth have you got?' to which another person might reply '500K'.) Strictly speaking, you are really referring to what's called the **baud rate** (or **baud**) when having a conversation like this! *You should note that this common usage would not be acceptable as a definition of bandwidth at A2 level.*

Bar code This is the system commonly seen on consumer goods in shops, where multiple lines having varying thickness represent a unique product code for anything from a 'book' to a 'can of beans'. Digits accompany the bar code so that humans can decode them without the need for a **bar code reader**, a **bar code scanner** or an **optical wand**.

Bar code reader This is the general name for a **bar code scanner** or **optical wand**.

Bar code scanner This is *a device which reads* **bar codes** by making use of a LASER beam. It can be permanently embedded into **Point Of Sale terminals** like those found at the supermarket, or may be a small hand-held portable device, like those used in libraries, for example.

Base class This is a concept used in **object-oriented programming**. This is *a* **class** *from which other classes may be derived*. Consider it to be like a blueprint from which similar 'plans' may be constructed. The use of class definitions cuts down development time on complex programs by a considerable amount.

Base index addressing This is a term used in **assembly language** programming which is a slight variation on **indexed addressing**. Consider the assembly language instruction 'mov cx, [bx + di]'. Here the base index register or 'bx register', is used as the base, and the destination index register, or di register, is use as an offset. In this way *an index is built up on the base* provided by the bx register, by *using the offset provided by the di register*. Hence the term base index addressing.

Base register addressing This is a term used in **assembly language** programming in which a base register, together with an **operand**, is used to provide the effective **address**. The assembly language instruction mov cx, [bx + 5] is an example, where the base register bx is used in conjunction with the operand 5 to place a number in the cx register.

Base ten The conventional *decimal* number system used for everyday arithmetic. It is also called **denary**.

Base two See **binary**.

Baseband This is a method of communication in which *only one particular frequency (***carrier frequency***) is used, and thus only one signal may be transmitted at any particular moment in time*. It is typical of the system used with **Ethernet**, the popular **LAN** technology. Compare with **broadband**.

BASIC This is the **high-level language** called *Beginner's All-purpose Symbolic Instruction Code*. The early versions of this language were unstructured and elementary, because they were designed to enable students who were not computer scientists to learn to program the computer. The latest version, like **Visual Basic.NET**, is now fully **object-oriented**, allowing the development of powerful applications. **Visual Basic** features one of the easiest to use front ends for designing **event-driven programs**.

Basic Input Output System When a computer is first switched on, it carries out instructions stored in the **BIOS** to **boot** the system. (It will, for example, perform 'checks on the hardware', load the 'configuration settings' stored in the **CMOS RAM**, and then load the **operating system**.) It is the BIOS that acts as an interface between different **hardware** configurations (types of **motherboard**) and the operating system on a computer. This is also called the **ROM BIOS**.

Batch This is basically a set of data that is treated as a *single consignment*. Any **batch processing** operation is carried out on the 'entire set' or batch of data. A **batch operating system** is usually needed to do this, under the guidance of the **job control language**. **Batch files** may also be run from **command line operating systems** such as **DOS**.

Batch file This is a **file** *containing one or more batch commands*. These commands could be typed manually into the **command line interpreter**, but instead are executed as a **batch** (one command being executed after the other) until the entire batch of commands contained within the batch file have been executed. A batch file is often generated by some automated process, and **software** like a **spreadsheet** could be used to create this file. It will need a secondary extension of (.bat) to work effectively on a **PC**. A batch file might typically be used to create 1,000 new users on a network, for example.

Batch operating system An **operating system** *designed* for **batch processing**. This is typical of the operating systems that would be present on a **minicomputer** or **mainframe computer** used by the utility companies or banks. In a batch operating system it is usual to give a series of commands to instruct the computer to do a particular job. After this command has been issued, the computer usually gets on with the job, and there is no extra interaction, unless errors occur. Typical of the operations carried out by a batch process would be clearing the millions of cheques that need to be processed each day by the clearing banks, or sending out hundreds of thousands of electricity bills. This type of operating system should be contrasted with an **interactive operating system**. See **job control language**.

Batch operation *Carrying out a sequence of identical processes*, normally on a large number of similar items. This is typical of the data processing that goes on in the utility billing industry, where thousands of customer records in a data file might have to be searched, the bills worked out and the invoices sent out each month.

Batch processing Processing data on a large number of items *one after the other* in the same session. Batch processing is typical of operations like cheques being cleared by the clearing banks or computers marking thousands of multiple-choice scripts using **mark sense reader** technology.

Batch total This is *used as a check on a particular* **batch** of data, usually to see if the entire batch has been processed properly i.e. no data is *missing*, *changed* or become *corrupted*. If, for example, we add up the number of transactions in a day to form a batch total, then this number could be used as a check when other information is being calculated on the same **transaction file**. E.g. going through and working out the total amount of V.A.T. due.

Baud This is a measure of the *information carrying capacity* of a communication channel. It is measured by the number of *state transitions* that take place each second which, in turn, represents a unit of information. A state transition can be something like a 'change in amplitude of the signal', represented by a 'different voltage', or a 'change in the angle of the signal relative to some reference' represented by a different 'phase'. It could also be a 'frequency change' in the signal, for example. This unit of information could be the 'code' or 'part of the code' representing a symbol like a 'letter' or 'number'. In very simple **modulation** systems, the **bit rate** and **baud rate** may be the same. In more complex modulation systems, like those used in modern **modems**, the baud rate can be much higher, because one baud can be used to represent more than one **bit**, and we therefore have more bits/sec, (bit rate) compared to the baud rate.

Baud rate This is the same as **baud**.

BCD See **Binary Coded Decimal**.

BCNF See **Backus Codd Normal Form**.

Bespoke software This is software that is written *specifically* for a particular client. Bespoke software enables the system to be tailored to the exact requirements of the client, and is often the only way to achieve certain things if a client's requirements are non standard. Bespoke software should be compared with **off-the-shelf software**, or **shrink wrapped software**.

Beta testing This is the *final stage of testing* before the real system is 'finished'. *Selected customers* (or everybody if a download is available on the **Internet**) *may be involved here*. The advantage is that customers get to use a piece of software for free, but the disadvantage is that the software may prove to be unreliable and even crash or 'damage' the user's machine. It is hoped that potential customers will report back **bugs** which are then fixed in a later beta release of the software. The advantage to the software manufacturer is they get their **software** tested under real conditions, and this enables them to see how it interacts with thousands of other commercial programs and different **hardware** configurations.

Binary This is the same as **base two**. It is a method of counting and performing arithmetic using only the digits '0' or '1'. However, other information like pictures and sound can also be encoded using binary. Indeed, everything inside the computer is ultimately coded in binary, because all programs must eventually be turned into **machine code**.

Binary Coded Decimal Binary Coded Decimal is a *convenient system* in which **binary** codes (four **bits** per digit) are used to represent each **decimal** digit. It is *not* a proper **number base**, but is often used when machines drive decimal digit displays or work in decimal. It is used because the conversion process from BCD to decimal and vice versa is extremely simple. For example, the BCD number 0011 0100 0001 would have a decimal equivalent of 3 4 1. If this were a pure **binary** number, the conversion to decimal would take much longer and be more complex.

Binary digit A zero, '0', or one, '1'. These are the only digits allowed in the **binary** system, and *all* **data** inside a computer is represented in this way.

Binary file *Binary files are files that contain data that can't easily be read in human readable form* (e.g. .exe files). Binary files usually need an appropriate program (like a word processor, spreadsheet or CAD package etc.) to read or make use of them, and if you load a binary file into a **text editor** you would probably see gobbledygook. This problem is particularly noticeable if you send **e-mail attachments** over the **Internet** making use of the **SMTP** system. The methods used by SMTP use only 7 bit **ASCII** code, and thus all the binary files must be converted into this form (using only 7 of the 8 bits available for each **byte**). This is achieved by using **MIME encoding**. On the PCs a suitable secondary file extension name is used to distinguish different types of binary and **text files**.

Binary number *A number made up from* **binary digits**. Binary numbers come in a variety of forms, including **integer fixed point**, **fractional fixed point** and **floating point** binary numbers.

Binary point This, just like the decimal point in a decimal number, is used to *separate the digits* representing *whole numbers* from the digits representing the *fractions*. Thus, the binary point separates the column headings ... 16, 8, 4, 2, 1 from the column headings 1/2, 1/4, 1/8, 1/16 etc.

Binary search *A method of searching an* **ordered list** in which the list is split into two parts (hence the term binary). If the item of interest is in the lower 'half' of the list then the top 'half' of the list is discarded, and the lower list is searched in the same way. This process is continued, operating on the lower list using the same methods, until the item of data is found, or found not to be in the list. This method is ideal for solution by using a technique called **recursion**.

Binary tree A **tree structure** in which the **parent nodes** are allowed a *maximum of two children* only. A binary tree is useful for storing ordered data which can be searched very quickly using a **binary search**.

BIOS See **Basic Input Output System**.

Bit See **Binary digit**. (Binary digIT.)

Bit-mapped graphic A graphic (*picture*) is made up from tiny dots called **pixels** (*Picture Elements*). A bit-mapped graphic will have jagged edges if you zoom into the image with a *large degree* of magnification, because the individual pixels will become visible. If the resolution of the picture is high, and the zoom level is not too great (1 : 1 preferably) then photographic quality is easily achieved. Bit-mapped graphics should be compared with the term **vector-based graphics**.

Bit rate The number of **bits** that are transmitted each second. This should be compared with the term **baud rate** or **baud**.

Black box testing *This is treating a system (or module) as though it were a black box*. This means that you don't need any knowledge of the code inside the 'box'. You simply know what inputs should produce particular outputs, and you don't really care how the system inside does this. As long as the right 'answers' come out when the appropriate inputs are entered, then the system can be successfully black-box tested. You should make use of appropriate **test data** to perform these tests.

Boolean A **data type** that can have only a *true* or *false* value.

Boot This is the act of *starting up a computer from switch on*, so that the **operating system** can be loaded. Once the operating system is loaded from **disk**, control is then passed over to it. A computer needs a program to execute at switch on, and the **bootstrap loader** is one of the first programs to execute once the **BIOS** configuration settings have been loaded and some basic hardware checks have been performed.

Bootstrap See **boot**.

Bootstrap loader A bootstrap loader is the part of the program in the **ROM BIOS** that executes enough code in the computer's memory to be able to load the **operating system** from **disk**. The term comes from the fact that you can help to pull your boots on by making use of your own boot straps. (American term for shoe laces!)

Bot This is the name given to a program whose job it is to find information on the **Internet**, or from private companies connected to the Internet. A typical function of a bot would be to gather suitable 'key word' information for **search engines**. A bot is also known as a **crawler** or a **spider**, but look at the term **agent** too.

Bottom up design This is a term used when designing **software** or systems. The bottom up approach to *design is useful for designing individual modules of a system which will be bolted together to form a larger system*. Typically modules may be designed and tested, and then not altered before being joined with other modules that have had similar treatment. This method of working is ideal when using **object-oriented programming** methods, where **base classes** can be used to define **objects** in the system, and other objects may be derived from them without altering the original code.

Boundary data This is the name given to **test data** which is either side of the limits of important values. An example would be choosing test data which was just below and just above **extreme data**. See also **erroneous data** and **normal data**.

Branch This is the *part of a* **tree structure** *which links two* **nodes**. The idea is identical in principle to a branch on a tree in the garden; hence the name.

Break point This is *a halt put into a program with the idea of helping to* **debug** *the code*. When the program is halted, the programmer will usually be able to inspect the state of different **variables** at the time the program was halted. This will usually help the programmer to find and cure any **bugs** in the program.

Bridge *A hardware device that can be used to connect two* **networks** (**LANs**) *together*, such as **Ethernet** and **Token ring**, for example. Some bridges can only connect together networks which share the same **protocols**. To connect networks using different protocols, a **gateway** or **managed hub** is sometimes used. An **intelligent bridge** can also be used to **segment** a network (i.e. to ensure that traffic keeps to a local segment, unless it needs to cross the bridge to another segment). This keeps network traffic to a minimum by preventing unnecessary traffic from travelling outside of the smaller segmented areas.

Bridging Connecting two different networks together via a **bridge**.

Broadband (1) The name given to a faster **Internet** connection when compared to a standard telephone link. Various speeds from a minimum of about 150 Kbit/sec (usually about 500 Kbits/sec) to 1 Mbit/sec or beyond constitute a broadband connection. Broadband makes use of technologies like **ADSL**.

Broadband (2) Broadband is a method of communication in which *different signals may be sent simultaneously over the same network link.* Different **carrier signal** frequencies are often used so that the multiple signals don't interfere with each other. Compare with the term **baseband**.

Brother node A **node** having other nodes on the same level in a **subtree**. (Same as a **sister node**.) A brother or sister node *must* share the same **parent node**.

Browser See **Internet browser**.

Bubble jet printer See **ink jet printer**.

Bubble sort This is an **algorithm** to sort data into order. *The bubble sort is a 4-stage process.* (1) Start off with the first pair of numbers in the unsorted list and compare. (2) If a swap is necessary set a flag. (3) Go onto the next pair of numbers, repeating stages (1) and (2). (4) When you have finished processing the list, if a swap took place, reset the flag and repeat the entire process again until the flag is not set, in which case the numbers are sorted. *Don't forget that the first 'pair of numbers' is represented by N(1) and N(2), and the next pair of numbers is represented by N(2) and N(3)* etc.

Buffer An area of **memory** set up to *temporarily* store data until it is needed. There are many different uses for a buffer, but typically a buffer would be used *to interface devices working at different speeds, to store data that might be waiting for a peripheral device*, and *to differentiate between the ways that software and hardware view* the **files** and **records** stored on a particular system.

Bug This is a *mistake* within a computer **program** or **algorithm**. It could be an *error* in the logic or **syntax** of a program. If errors occur with electronic components on a piece of computer **hardware**, then it's usually called a *fault*.

Built-in data type This is a **data type** that is built in to a **programming language** or **application**. Typical built-in data types might be **integer**, **real**, **string** and **array** etc. In some languages programmers may define their own data types.

Bus See **bus system**.

Bus system The *parallel group of wires* that connect components and **peripherals** inside a computer system. There are bus systems inside the **microprocessor**, etched onto the **motherboard** and brought out by cables to devices such as **disks** and **printers**. There are *three main bus systems* called the **address bus**, **data bus** and **control bus**.

Bus topology In **network topology**, a system where all the computers on the bus **network** are connected to the *same linear communications channel*, usually with a terminator at each end. All computers detect the data on the bus, but only those for which the data is intended pay any attention to it. If more than one computer tries to communicate at *exactly* the same moment in time, a **collision** will occur, and the data will need to be retransmitted after a very short time period.

Byte Eight **binary digits**. This is *a fundamental unit of the measurement of storage capacity*. In the **ASCII** system a byte represents a single character, but more recently the **Unicode** system uses two bytes.

C++ This is a **high-level language**. It is a fully **object-oriented programming language**, used for development of very powerful **applications** and **operating systems**. It is also useful for teaching the concepts of object-oriented programming.

Cache memory This is *fast* **memory** that can be used to hold the contents of data that is likely to be needed *very quickly* (i.e. instructions that might soon be executed by the **microprocessor**.) Because cache is faster than normal memory, the effect is to *speed up the operation of the computer*.

CAD See **Computer Aided Design**.

CAD package **Software** which enables complex 2D and 3D **computer graphics** to be created. High-end CAD packages will also perform operations like **rendering**, and **animation**. Industrial **CAD** packages will also link to **Computer Aided Manufacture** (CAM) systems.

CAL See **Computer Aided Learning**.

CAM See **Computer Aided Manufacture**.

Candidate key When designing a **relational database**, *a candidate key is a key that could be used to uniquely define a record*. It is therefore an **attribute** that is a *possible alternative to the* **primary key**.

Carrier frequency The frequency of the **carrier signal** in a transmission system – it is measured in cycles/second.

Carrier signal A signal that is used to carry the actual data or information. This carrier signal is usually modulated in some way so that the information is transmitted on the back of the carrier signal. A large number of different **modulation** methods are available, depending on the complexity of the system.

Carry *The bit generated from a sum when carrying data to the next column*. A **bit** representing the **carry flag** in the **flag register** usually indicates if this has happened inside a **microprocessor**.

Carry flag A **bit** inside the **flag register** used to indicate that a **carry** has occurred.

CASE Computer Aided Software Engineering. This is **software** that *provides a variety of functions for the development and testing of software*. Typically this might include help with design, coding, testing (especially **white box testing**), **prototyping** and planning.

Case statement A **program statement** which is designed to replace multiple line if-then statements.

CAT standard This is a set of standards (CAT 3 or CAT 5, for example) used for unshielded **twisted pair** cables like those used in **Ethernet networks**. To conform to a particular standard special cables have to be purchased, terminated properly with the right connectors, and then installed without damage to ensure that the theoretical **bandwidth** is actually achieved in practice.

CBT See **Computer Based Training**.

CD See **Compact Disc**.

CD-R See **Compact Disc Recordable**.

CD-ROM See **Compact Disc Read Only Memory**.

CD-RW See **Compact Disc Re-Writable**.

Central Processing Unit This is *the part of a computer system used for executing* **machine code** *instructions, performing calculations and carrying out other operations*. On **mainframe** and **supercomputers** there are usually many **microprocessors** housed in a special cabinet. However, on a typical **microcomputer** it is usually housed inside a single microprocessor chip.

CGI See **Common Gateway Interface**.

CGI script Normal **HTML** pages are static; this means that no information can be gathered from the users when surfing with their **browser** on the **Internet**. *When using a CGI script, data typed in by the user may be sent back to the* **web server**. *The CGI script can process this data at the server end, and then send it back to the user's browser*. Thus, entries destined for a **database** on a file server, for example, can be confirmed to the users by the CGI script returning appropriate data. Other ways of doing similar things would be by using **VBScript** or **Active server pages**, for example.

Character set The *set of characters used by a particular system* like **ASCII**, **extended ASCII**, **Unicode**, or the characters used in some programming language, for example. The character set typically consists of 'upper and lower case letters', 'numbers', 'punctuation' and other 'special characters' like 'control codes' and 'foreign punctuation' etc.

Check digit This is used as a *check* on the **integrity** of a *single number*. It is ideal for checking account numbers or customer ID numbers, for example. Only one digit needs to be stored along with the original number to get a high confidence rating on the integrity of a newly entered or recently transmitted account number.

Checksum A checksum is a way of generating a number which attempts to ensure the **integrity** of stored or transmitted data. It could be calculated on a block of data by adding together the **bytes** or words (**ASCII** values), and then storing the result in a limited number of **bits** (we ignore any **overflow** that might occur). The methods of calculating the checksum might vary, but as long as the *same*

algorithm is used at both ends of the transmission system it does not matter. Some algorithms are better than others, and the data to be transmitted might determine the methods to be used.

Child node An item of data in a **tree structure** that has a **parent node** (the node from which it is derived on the level above).

CIR See **Current Instruction Register**.

Circuit switching A *dedicated line* is established for as long as is necessary, even if no information is being transmitted at any particular moment of time. Compare this with **message switching**, which only establishes a communication line for the duration of the **message**. See also **packet switching**.

Circular queue A **data structure** based on the **FIFO** principle in which the beginning and end of the **queue** are implemented by **pointers**. When using a circular queue a limited number of memory elements are assigned to the queue, and a *round-robin technique* is used so that space at the beginning of the queue does not remain permanently vacant when data items have been removed. The beginning and end pointers enable the **programmer** to keep tabs on where the queue starts and ends.

Class A *class is an* **abstract data type**, *and can be thought of as a blueprint or definition*. Classes are self-contained structures and are used in **object-oriented programming** languages to define a data type used to create an **object**, which is a particular instance (or example) of a class. A class may *control access to the methods and data contained within it* by using mechanisms like **encapsulation**, and carries out this control by making use of keywords like **public**, **private** and **protected**.

Class A network This is a **network** in which the first **bit** of the **IP address** starts off with a 0, and the *first byte* of the IP address is used to define the **network ID**. Thus the remaining 3 bytes of the IP address are used to define the hosts or **Host IDs**. Using these number patterns and the first byte we can thus theoretically define 128 networks [(00000000) to (01111111)] and, using the last three bytes [2^{24}] 16,777,215 hosts. However, not all addresses in this range are necessarily used in this way.

Class attributes This is a term used in **object-oriented analysis**. *Class attributes are characteristics belonging to a particular class*. As an example, in an **object-oriented programming language**, a **class**, 'Computer', may have **attributes**, 'Software', 'Processor', 'Motherboard', 'Memory' and 'Disk Drive' etc. *In other words the class attributes are the 'data or information' that should be known by the class.* Information belonging to a class is shown on a **class diagram** using a square box made up from three compartments. *The class attributes are written in the middle compartment*, which shows the **encapsulated** attributes by name, together with a variety of 'symbols' representing properties like **public**, **private** and **protected**, for example. There are several others, but a '–' sign in front of an attribute indicates that it is private, a '+' sign in front of an attribute indicates that it is public, and a '#' sign indicates that it is protected. See also **object-oriented analysis** and **object analysis diagram**.

Class B network This is a **network** in which the first two **bits** of the **IP address** start off with 10, and the *first two bytes* of the IP address are used to define the **network ID**. Thus the remaining 2 bytes of the IP address are used to define the hosts or Host IDs. Using these number patterns and the first two bytes we can thus theoretically define 16,383 networks [(10000000 00000000) to (10111111 11111111)] and, using the last two bytes [2^{16}] 65,536 hosts. However, not all addresses in this range are necessarily used in this way.

Class C network This is a **network** in which the first three **bits** of the **IP address** start off with 110, and the *first three bytes* of the IP address are used to define the **network ID**. Thus the remaining 1 byte of the IP address is used to define the hosts or Host IDs. Using these number patterns and the first three bytes we can thus theoretically define 2,097,151 networks [(11000000 00000000 00000000) to (11011111 11111111 11111111)] and, using the last byte [2^{8}] 256 hosts. However, not all addresses in this range are necessarily used in this way.

Class D network This is a **network** in which the first four **bits** of the **IP address** start off with 1110. These networks are used for multicasting. This means sending information simultaneously to many computers, and is useful when a disk image of a machine needs to be sent to many others, for example.

Class diagram This type of diagram is useful for undertaking an **object-oriented analysis** of a problem *before* any **object-oriented programs** are designed or written. *Class diagrams are the foundation of the pictorial methods* (see **UML**) *on which object-oriented analysis is based. A class diagram is a pictorial method of showing classes and the relationships that exist between them*. Classes are drawn inside a rectangular box consisting of three compartments, and the **relationships** are shown by different sorts of annotated lines and arrows connecting the boxes. The name of the **class** is written in the top compartment, the **class attributes** are written in the middle compartment and the **class operations** are written in the bottom compartment. If you are undertaking an A2 project involving an object-oriented language like **C++**, **Java** or **Visual Basic.NET**, then you should have this type of diagram in the **analysis** section of your project. See also **object-oriented analysis** and **object analysis diagram**.

Class E network This is a **network** in which the first four **bits** of the **IP address** start off with 1111. These networks are used for experimental purposes.

Class operations This is a term used in **object-oriented analysis**. The term 'operations' is used in **Java**, but these operations are called **methods** in the language **C++**. **Operations** *are therefore the routines like* **functions** *and* **procedures** *to be carried out by a* **class**. Class operations may be shown on a **class diagram**, which details the 'actions' or the 'manipulation of attributes'. A class is represented by a square box split into three compartments, and the final (bottom compartment) contains the operations or methods to be carried out by the class. The class name is written in the top compartment, and the **class attributes** are written in the middle compartment. If you are undertaking an A2 project involving an **object-oriented language** like **C++**, **Java** or **Visual Basic.NET**, then you should have this type of diagram in the **analysis** section of your project. See also **object-oriented analysis** and **object analysis diagram**.

Classic system life cycle See **system life cycle**.

Clause A term used in **logic programming** such as **Prolog**. In Prolog, for example, the program is made up from a number of clauses, each terminated by a full stop. At A2 level *you do not need to know the logical definition of this term*, which includes concepts like 'conjunctions', 'disjunctions' and 'assertions' etc.

CLI See **Command Line Interface**.

Client (1) The name given to a **workstation** connected to a **LAN**.

Client (2) The person or people for whom you are designing your **A2 project**. It is important to have a *real client* so that you can build up a sensible set of project **objectives** and get feedback throughout the duration of your project work.

Client server network This is a form of **distributed processing** where *a client* (e.g. a computer on a **network**) *works in conjunction with a network* **file server**. It is usual to have many servers and a huge number of clients operating in this mode, where any client may access one or more servers simultaneously.

Clock The *electronic signal* derived from a crystal on the **motherboard**. It is used for initiating the **fetch-decode-execute cycle** and for other synchronisation purposes like internal data transmission.

CMOS RAM The **RAM** chip which *stores the settings* for the **BIOS**. It does this by having a small battery on the **motherboard** which keeps this chip powered when the computer is switched off. It is *not* part of the BIOS itself, because the BIOS is stored on **ROM** or **flash ROM**. However, the BIOS does use the settings in the CMOS RAM to *configure the machine* correctly in terms of **hardware**, like the number and type of disks actually present, for example.

CMYK This is the subtractive colour system used for printing. Cyan, Magenta, Yellow and Key (Black) are used to produce the colours on the printed page. See **subtractive primary colours**.

CNC See **Computer Numeric Control**.

Coaxial cable A cable in which *both conductors share the same axis*. One cable is in the middle and a concentric cable runs around the outside. This is commonly used for Lowband **Ethernet** (10 Mbit/sec), for radio, TV and satellite signals.

COBOL Common Business Oriented Language. A **high-level language** ideally suited for business transactions in banking and commerce.

Code sharing See **re-entrant code**.

CODEC This stands for COder/DECoder. It is a device (or **software**) that *encodes* or *decodes* the data. Characters recognised by humans, for example, may be encoded into **ASCII** form for transmission over a communication link. At the other end of the link, the ASCII codes would need to be decoded so that the message is turned back into human-readable characters. Software CODECS are used extensively to compress and decompress data such as sound and images when being transmitted over networks like the Internet. Typical examples of these CODECS are MPEG and WMA Audio.

Collision In a **baseband network**, this is *the state that happens when two computers simultaneously try to use the same communications channel*. If this happens, the two computers wait for a very short period of random time and then try again. On very busy networks, especially if the **bandwidth** is *insufficient* for the amount of traffic, many collisions occur; the network becomes slow and ceases to be effective. A system like the **token ring** eliminates collisions altogether.

COM This is an **acronym** for Computer Output on Microform. It is the collective term for **microfilm** and **microfiche**.

Comma Separated Value A means of *importing* and *exporting* data between **applications** by using the data to be imported or exported (the *values*) separated by *commas*.

Command driven One way of providing *interaction* with a user where commands are typed into the computer. **DOS**, Microsoft's **Disk Operating System** is a good example of a command-driven system.

Command Line Interface That part of a **command line operating system** which consists of a command prompt (e.g. it could be 'c:\>' in **DOS** or '$' in **Unix**). It is a non-graphical interface into which the user has to type in a set of commands which are not very user friendly. Compare with a **GUI**, which is much easier to use.

Command line interpreter This is the name of the *software* that takes commands from the **Command Line Interface** presented by a **command line operating system** and interprets them (i.e. checks the **syntax** and, if 'correct', carries out the requests that the user has just typed in).

Command line operating system In this type of **operating system** the user typically types in commands, rather than operating through a **GUI**. Microsoft's **DOS** is a good example of a **command line operating system** where commands like 'C:' would be needed to make the C drive the current designated drive, or 'DIR D:' would be one of the commands to list the **files** and **directories** on the D drive.

Comments In a programming language, this means *adding text to help explain what the program does*. The text is physically part of the actual program, but the **compilers** or **interpreters** pay no attention to them. Good use of comments aids **documentation**, and should be used to ensure good **structured programming** style.

Commissioning This is the *installation phase*, when a new computer system is installed at a customer's site. Extensive **testing** should have gone into the system already, but commissioning a system makes sure that it's working to the customer's satisfaction. After commissioning, it may still be necessary to maintain the system at a later stage, and this is called **maintenance**.

Commissioning engineer A highly competent technical person who helps to **commission** (set up) a brand new computer system.

Common Gateway Interface Typically this is one of the methods used to access **databases** on an **Internet server**, and present data to the user in a **browser** using an **HTML** page. More generally, *CGI is a method for linking external applications to* **web servers**. Programs that use this method are written in **CGI script**. Running CGI scripts can be dangerous, because they are executing on a client machine. A special directory on your computer is used for this purpose, and special security settings have to be set up too.

Communication requirements of a system This term is used when performing a **systems analysis**. The 'communication requirements of a system' deal with the user interface. It thus concentrates on different methods of inputting data, different input devices that might be used and different types of screen displays etc. See **system life cycle**.

Communications network The *transmission channels* (e.g. **LAN**s, **WAN**s) connecting computers together so that they may exchange information and share resources.

Compact Disc See **Compact Disc Read Only Memory** (**CD-ROM**).

Compact Disc Read Only Memory This is a *read-only device* that is common for the distribution of **software**. It can hold about 650 **Mbytes** of data, and is thus very cost effective, because the media is inexpensive.

Compact Disc Recordable This disc can be *written to just once*, but *can* be read by an ordinary **CD-ROM** drive. Compare this with **CD-RW** or **Compact Disc Re-Writable**.

Compact Disc Re-Writable This disc can be reused many times, but *can't* be read in a conventional **CD-ROM** drive. To read these discs you either use the drive that was used to record them, or one of the multi-read format **CD** or **DVD** drives.

Compiler **Software** that converts a **high-level language** into **machine code**. It does this by creating the **object code** which is to be run on the target machine. If any errors are found during the compilation process, then the **source code** will have to be recompiled. A **compiler** should be compared with an **interpreter**. Do *not* confuse this with an **assembler**.

Composite key field See **key field**.

Composite primary key When designing a **relational database**, this is a **primary key** *which is made up from more than one* **attribute** or **field**. A composite primary key is sometimes needed to make the **primary key** unique. Typically an 'order number – item number' combination might be used as a composite primary key. Relational databases like Microsoft's Access allow you to choose multiple attributes to define a composite primary key in this way.

Computer A computer is a processor of data. After structure has been applied to data, it becomes **information**. Information that has been processed forms the basis of knowledge itself. A computer is *the most general purpose machine* that man has invented to date.

Computer Aided Design This is when computers are used to help with the design and manufacturing process. Typically **CAD packages** are used to help design and build virtually any artefact from 'aircraft' to a 'mug for drinking coffee'. See also **CAD package**.

Computer Aided Learning Computer Aided Learning or Computer Assisted Learning is software specifically designed to teach a subject by making use of the computer. It will usually guide the student through the principles, offer examples for the student to complete, and maybe offer tests at the end to see how well the student has done. Such programs are usually developed by means of an **authoring package**.

Computer Aided Manufacture This is the use of computers to aid in the *construction of artefacts* such as automobiles, aircraft, computers and most other objects that can be built in a factory specially set up for this purpose.

Computer Based Training See **Computer Aided Learning**.

Computer graphics These are pictures drawn on a computer. There are usually two basic types of pictures, or image, called **pixel-based graphics** or **vector-based graphics**.

Computer Misuse Act Legislation to ensure that criminals can be punished under the law for 'hacking', 'injection of viruses' or similar illegal activities. The specific offences are *'Unauthorised access to computer material'*, *'Unauthorised access with intent to commit or facilitate commission of further offence'* and *'Unauthorised modification of computer material'*. You can download a copy of this act from the **Internet**.

Computer Numeric Control This is the technology used by computers to control machines like lathes and milling machines etc., which manufacture mechanical or electronic components and equipment. Numbers generated by computers precisely control the position of the tools, the type of tools (drill size etc.) and the actions taken by the tool with little intervention from the human operator. It is possible to generate the numerical information to control these machines from **CAD packages**, which are used by the engineers and designers of the artefacts.

Computer program See **program**.

Concept keyboard This is a **keyboard** in which an *overlay* can be used to change the functionality of the keys. It is used extensively in primary schools where pictures can be placed over the keyboard, enabling children to press keys with special pictures or other characters on them. They may then interact with the computer in ways *depending on the* **software** that is running at the time. Many concept keyboards have much bigger keys than those found on a normal keyboard.

Conceptual level This is a view of a **relational database** from the point of view of the **database administrator**. The conceptual level would include views of the database **tables**, **queries**, setting up the database **relationships** and **normalisation** etc.

Conceptual schema The conceptual or **logical schema** is the *description* of a **relational database**. The **data definition language** is used to provide this description of the structure of the database, and thus completely describes the conceptual model (hence the name) of the database. It's therefore *the* **entities**, **attributes** and **relationships** *that make up the structure of the relational database*.

Concurrent access This is a **database** term referring to different users *accessing the same information at the same moment in time*. If a particular record is put into read-only mode, then it's acceptable for any number of people to access information within it, but *if the data can be altered by different people simultaneously, then an* **exclusive lock** *must be put on a particular record*, usually by the first person to access the data. If this is not done then two or more people might try to alter the same data simultaneously, leading to errors or a great deal of confusion. An exclusive lock is also known as **record locking**.

Conditional jump This is a term normally associated with **assembly language**. *Control may be passed to a different part of the program based on some particular condition*, e.g. *jump* if a particular **flag** is set. It is similar in principle to the 'if then' instruction used in some **high-level languages**.

Constant A value in a **program** that is *not allowed to change*. This should be contrasted with a **variable**, whose value is allowed to change while the program is being executed. A constant may be declared at the beginning of a program by using a program statement like 'Const start = 6, finish = 20', which in **Visual Basic** declares the variables 'start' and 'finish' as constants, and sets up their values to be 6 and 20 respectively. *Meaningful names* should be used for constants to promote good **structured programming** style.

Continuous stationery A **fan-fold paper** system that feeds into the printer in a continuous form (i.e. each page is joined onto the previous page in a zigzag fashion). This is popular in businesses that have large stock lists to print out.

Control bus The group of wires along which **data** representing the **control signals** pass.

Control codes **ASCII** codes (or other codes like **EBCDIC**) used for *special purposes* like a 'Line Feed', 'Carriage Return' or 'Escape'. There are many non-printable control codes used for a variety of *control* purposes.

Control signal A signal which indicates some form of control, like instructing the **memory** to perform a *read* (getting data from the memory) or a *write* (putting data into the memory) operation or synchronising devices with the **clock**. Control signals also help to control **peripherals**.

Control structure In a **programming language**, a structure like 'DO WHILE' or 'IF THEN ELSE' etc. used to *control the order* in which **program statements** might be executed.

Control total This is a check on the **integrity** of **data**. A control total is usually made up from some *suitable selection of data items* in the data to be stored or transmitted. It can be as simple as a meaningful total on some numeric field, or it can be more complex. For example, it could be the 'number of lines in an invoice' + 'total amount for the invoice' + 'consignment number'. This number is then sent along (or stored) with the data, and the same calculations performed at the receiving end. *If a discrepancy has occurred, then the control total is likely to be different*, in which case the document or invoice etc. has been tampered with. Different companies would have their own methods of calculating the control total, and the ideas are virtually identical to the **hash totals** used when transmitting data.

Control unit The unit *inside* a **microprocessor** which controls operations like instructing the **ALU** to perform an 'ADD' operation or deciding if data needs to be moved from one **register** to another.

Conversion This is the name given to the process of *converting an old system to a new one*. It is a term often used by **systems analysts** when implementing a computerised system.

Cookies Some **web servers** store *information about users on the client machine*. This can often speed up log on to certain sites, or help set parameters that are customised to a particular user. Typically they might be used such that each time a particular site is visited, the user can get pages and/or other information based on their previous preferences.

Copyright Design and Patents Act This is legislation to *protect intellectual property*. Under this act, if you wish to copy or use **software**, then permission must be sought from the appropriate authorities. Patents prevent *identical* or *very similar* products or ideas being copied by other people trying to present them as their own. You can download a copy of this act from the Internet.

CPU See **Central Processing Unit**.

Crawler See **bot**.

CRC See **Cyclic Redundancy Check**.

Credit card A card (like Barclaycard, MasterCard and Amex) on which **transactions**, up to a certain limit (your *credit limit*), are allowed. The bill is then settled by monthly instalments. This should be compared with a **debit card**.

Cross tabulation For the purposes of A2 computing, this is a way of producing a **query** in a **database** that allows the user to *summarise large amounts of data based on some conditions*. You could, for example, have two fields representing the rows and columns like a spreadsheet, and have a third field which provides the data to fill in the 'cells'. Microsoft Access has a cross tab query wizard which is relatively easy to use.

CSV See **Comma Separated Value**.

Current instruction The instruction *currently being executed* by a **microprocessor**. This instruction is usually stored in the **current instruction register**.

Current Instruction Register This is *the* **register** where the **current instruction** (the instruction just fetched from main memory) *is placed*. The binary patterns representing the current instruction may therefore be decoded by the **microprocessor** by inspection of the **bits** within this **register**.

Cyclic Redundancy Check This is a very sophisticated **error-detection** mechanism that is used when information is sent over a communications **network**. The message is split up into a suitable number of small chunks like a **packet**, and a **CRC** check (similar idea to a **checksum**) is added to the transmitted data. The binary data is processed by using mathematical polynomials, and methods of division produce a remainder which gets used as the CRC digits. Although it sounds complex, computers can perform these polynomial division calculations in an instant, and nobody will notice any significant delay. CRC methods using polynomials are popular because the rate of detection of errors is very much higher than using other methods like **check digits** and checksums.

DAC See **digital to analogue converter**.
DAT See **digital audio tape**.
Data *Raw data* is the basic material on which a **computer** operates. Once data has been **decoded**, has 'format and context' added and is 'output to the user', it then becomes **information**. 'Information = data + structure' is often used to express this. The term data is used as both singular and plural in the computer industry.
Data bus The *parallel group of wires* along which the **binary digits** representing the data travel, in both directions. **Data** is usually moved between the **microprocessor**, **memory** and **peripherals** by travelling along the data bus.
Data capture form *A special form designed for the manual capture of data*. It is usually used to gather data which will be inputted to the computer at a later stage. A typical example of a data capture form could be a 'sales contract' used by a double-glazing salesman to sell windows. This form would have details like 'customer name and address', 'telephone number', 'number of windows', 'type of windows' and 'cost' etc. All this gathered information might then be taken back to the office and entered into the computer system by looking at the data capture form.
Data consistency This is a general term, but is frequently applied to **databases**, which defines how a well-designed database should operate, in terms of correct **data entry** procedures, proper **data processing** and well-defined data output procedures. As an example, a badly-designed database, in which identical data items were entered differently (e.g. a company name might be spelt differently in different places), would hold *inconsistent data*. Well-designed databases should ensure that errors like these do not occur, thus ensuring *good data consistency*.
Data control language This *is the part of* **SQL** *that provides the security* in a **relational database**. The **DBA** may control 'who has access to what' via commands such as 'GRANT' and 'REVOKE'.
Data definition language This is *the part of* **SQL** *that allows the* **DBA** *to create the* **relational database**. As an example, the **DDL** could be used for the creation of relational database tables, and allow the restructuring of the database after it has been created. Typical SQL commands for a DDL might be 'CREATE TABLE' and 'CREATE INDEX'.
Data description language See **data definition language**.
Data dictionary (1) This is *data about data*. For example, we may have a list, showing **attributes** about an **entity** in a database **table**. A library **database**, for example, might have an 'author entry' in the data dictionary. Alongside this **field** name the data dictionary might have entries like '25 characters long', have a **data type** of 'text', be 'a required field' and require no **validation**.
Data dictionary (2) In an **RDBMS** the data dictionary is hidden from the user because it defines how the **DBMS** integrates with the data. The data dictionary is important because without this **file** the database would not be able to access any data.
Data entry The process of entering data into a computer system. The methods of data entry are vast, and include **keyboards**, **scanners**, **OCR systems**, **MICR readers**, voice etc. Good data entry routines should ensure that any *errors are kept to a minimum* via the use of techniques such as **validation**, **verification**, **batch totals**, **check digits** and **checksums** etc.
Data flow diagram This is a diagram, useful in **systems development** for showing how **information** moves around a system in a variety of forms. There *are four different data flow symbols*, namely a *data processing symbol*, a *source and destination symbol*, a *data storage symbol* and an *arrow* connecting the other symbols. Data flow diagrams are excellent not only for showing the movement of data within a computer system, but also the movement of data in a manual system (the flow of paperwork moving around an office, for example.)
Data flow symbols These are the symbols used on a **data flow diagram**, namely '*arrows*' to show the direction of the data flow, '*data processing symbols*', '*storage of data symbols*' and '*source or destination of data symbols*'.
Data glove *This is a glove, worn over the hand, which detects the movements of the hand (within a defined space) and the movements of the fingers (like degree of bending etc.)*. With appropriate **software** and powerful computers it is thus possible to interact with virtual objects in a virtual world. Virtual musical instruments have been played by this method, and virtual objects have been lifted by more than one person, each cooperating from different remote locations via the **Internet**.
Data integrity (1) In a communication system, *ensuring that transmitted data is still correct after it has been received* i.e. making sure that it has not become corrupted due to some error in the transmission system. This is achieved through techniques like **parity** and **CRCs**.
Data integrity (2) The term is also used *more generally* to ensure that data is complete, correct and not corrupted in any way, and is used quite

frequently when data is processed by a **database**. When designing a **database**, **validation** and **verification** are two methods of helping to maintain data integrity.

Data link layer This is *layer two* of the **ISO OSI model**. The data link layer splits up the signal into frames ready to be sent over the **physical layer**. The data link layer links the physical layer to the **network layer**, and provides extra functionality such as synchronisation and detecting errors in data transmission.

Data logger This is a device designed to *interface* a variety of **sensors** to a computer system. Data loggers are ideal for collecting data from scientific experiments, or for measuring pollution before the data is analysed by a computer. Some data loggers need to be permanently connected to a computer, but others may be used remotely, and the data collected and downloaded into the computer system at a later stage.

Data manipulation language This is the *part of* **SQL** *that allows a user to manipulate data in the* **relational database**. As an example, it would be possible to update tables, by allowing addition and deletion of data. Typical SQL commands for a DML are 'INSERT' and 'DELETE'.

Data processing This is the name usually given to *the processes that go on in a typical business* where data is generated and processed each day, and the results stored in **files** and **databases** held on computers. *All* computers obviously process data, whatever they are doing! However, typical examples of an *appropriate use of this term* would be the data processing carried out by the 'banks', 'retail industries', 'utility companies' and other similar institutions.

Data Protection Act This is legislation to *protect individuals* from misuse of information held about them on a computer. The act can be summarised by the following few points:
the data should be processed fairly and lawfully;
the data should not be used for any other purpose;
the data shall be adequate and relevant;
the data shall be accurate and kept up to date;
the data shall not be kept for longer than necessary;
the data shall be protected from unauthorised access;
the data shall not be transferred outside the EEC unless the country concerned complies with the act;
the person about whom the data is stored must have given their consent.

Data query language This is the *part of* **SQL** *that allows users to make queries on the data in a* **relational database**. As an example, it would be possible to find out what records within the database match certain criteria. Typical SQL commands for the DQL are 'SELECT', together with supporting commands like 'FROM' and 'WHERE'.

Data requirements This is part of the **design** of your **A2 project** where you are expected to identify **data** to be input into the system and the data to be output from the system. This could include the type of data (**string**, **integer**, **floating point** etc.), from where it is obtained (e.g. **data capture form**) and the ways in which the data will be output (a **report** from a **database**), for example. The format of the data could be important too, such as the total number of characters permitted or whether there are any special requirements like leading capital letters or special date formats.

Data security This is making sure that the **data** in a computer system is *kept safe* from **hackers** or other forms of unauthorised or illegal access, system failure, fire, pestilence and floods etc. The methods of doing this might involve physical locks on the computer room doors, and the use of **passwords**, and **encryption** of data etc.

Data sharing This is a term applied to *sharing data between different users and applicatons* when using applications like a **database**, for example. It is not as simple as it might appear at first sight, because different people might be attempting to *update* the same record at the same time. To get over this, **record locking** is usually used.

Data structures Data structures are ways of modelling particular processes like **Queues**, **Stacks**, **Arrays**, **Heaps** and **Trees**. Each of these data structures enables the data contained within it to be treated as a *single entity*, and thus be processed efficiently by a computer. These and other data structures are used in computer science to help solve common problems, and *students should learn when it is appropriate* to use a particular type of data structure. See also **abstract data types**.

Data type A specific category of **data** in a **computer program** or **application**. This category defines the type of data that can be used and the range which particular data may take on. Examples of typical built-in data types are **integer**, **floating point**, **Boolean**, **string** and **array**, but many **high-level programming languages** enable the user to define their own data types too. See **built-in data type**.

Data validation See **validation**.

Database This is a collection of data *organised in such a way* that information may be *stored efficiently*, *retrieved very easily* by using **queries** *and output attractively* using **reports**. The **relational database** is the most popular, but **object-oriented databases** are gaining much prominence.

Database administrator This is *the person who is in charge of setting up a* **DBMS**. Such a person must be highly responsible, as they are given the highest level of privilege and can view any data within a **database**. They are usually responsible for setting up the database **schema**, and therefore for designing the entire database.

Database management system This is software designed to store and manage databases. It is the *conceptual level* of the three-level **DBMS** architecture, which consists of the highest level (**users' view**), the **conceptual level** (the DBMS) and the lowest level (physical data stored on disk). If a **relational database** management system is used then this is often known as the **RDBMS**.

Database server A **file server** on which a **database** is hosted. The database is usually accessed by client machines in a **client server** network on a **LAN** or from a **browser** being used on the **Internet**.

Datagram When a **packet** of data is transmitted, *along with other information like destination address*, it is known as a datagram. It is therefore a packet of information, set up so that it may be routed from one place to another on a **network** like an **intranet** or the **Internet**. The datagram is completely self contained, and is routed by having its **destination** address examined by computers or other equipment (like **bridges**, **switches** and **gateways** etc.) designed to help with routing.

Daughter board A board that plugs into the **motherboard**, specifically to interface peripheral devices like **video cards**, **sound cards**, **graphics cards** and many others. It plugs into a variety of **bus systems** depending on the type of board.

DBA See **Database administrator**.

DBMS See **Database management system**.

DCL See **Data control language**.

DDL See **Data definition language**.

Debit card A card which normally *debits money directly from your bank account*. A typical example is Maestro. This should be compared with a **credit card** (such as Barclaycard or MasterCard) on which credit is available, that can then be paid off by monthly instalments.

Debugging The *process of finding errors*, usually in a **program** or some other **algorithm**. Most **high-level languages** support **interfaces** which provide a variety of debugging tools. Typical of these would be single stepping through the code and the insertion of **break points**.

Declaration This is the *act* of declaring (making the computer aware of) things like **variables** and **constants**. In programming this is carried out by special **program statements**. In some languages declaration is also used to declare **procedures** and **functions** too. It forces the programmer to think about the variables and constants being used, and the procedures and functions that are needed. This helps considerably with good **structured programming** style.

Declarative language This is a **high-level language** which does *not* rely on imperatives, but on defining **facts** and **rules** to build up a **knowledge base** which can then be interrogated. A **high-level language** like **Prolog** is an example of a declarative language. A declarative language should be compared with an **imperative programming language**.

Decode (1) *Interpreting the meaning of a pattern of binary digits* (in the case of the **fetch-decode-execute cycle**).

Decode (2) Changing from one coding system into another, usually **machine readable** into **human readable**. The opposite of decoding is **encoding**.

Decoding Changing **encoded data** back into its original form. E.g. changing **ASCII** or **Unicode** back into recognisable text. The term is frequently applied to changing data from **machine readable** form into **human readable** form.

Dedicated register This is a **register**, normally resident inside a **microprocessor**, which is *dedicated to a particular task*. Typical examples are the **program counter** or **sequence control register**, dedicated to the task of keeping the place in **main memory** from where the next instruction is to be fetched, or the **memory data register**, which holds the current program instruction or **data** just written to or read from main memory.

Defaults A set of *sensible values* used when no other information is specified. E.g. if a numeric **variable** has not been set up within a **program**, then its default value might be assumed to be zero.

Defragmented A **disk** (*or memory*) becomes fragmented after it has been in use for some time. Space allocated to old programs gets released for new programs when the old ones are no longer needed, but the new programs don't fit into the old spaces, and thus get stored on the disk in a less efficient way. Accessing the data that is spread out over the disk like this becomes very slow, especially if the disk is badly fragmented. A **disk defragmenter utility** can be run to overcome this problem.

Delphi The *visual version of* **Pascal**. This is Borland's answer to Microsoft's **Visual Basic**. A programming front end, similar to that provided for Visual Basic is used to write Pascal programs and thus develop powerful applications.

Demodulation The process of *extracting information* from a signal that has previously been converted (**modulated**) into a form for transmission over a communication link. E.g. converting a **digital signal** back into a voice signal so that it can be understood by humans.

Denary The same as **Base ten** or Decimal, the number system in everyday use.

Dependencies This is a term used in **object-oriented analysis**, and describes one sort of **relationship**. Dependencies are relationships which show the **associations** between two **classes** or **objects** *where one is a collection of dependent elements and the other is a collection of independent elements*. The dependent elements will require knowledge of the independent elements to carry out their functions, and so a dependency relationship is needed. *These dependencies are typically not persistent, and are therefore shown by a dotted arrow instead of using a solid line between the boxes that represent the classes or objects. The arrow head points to the independent elements.* As an example, you might be modelling some route planning software, and a report on a requested route might be output to the printer, which could then be discarded (i.e. the information built up is not persistent). See also **object-oriented analysis** and **object analysis diagrams**.

Derived class This is a concept used in **object-oriented programming**. *A derived class can inherit properties from the* **base class** by the mechanism of **inheritance**. The properties that can be inherited are controlled by the base class, but new properties and methods may be added to the derived class. Using derived classes cuts down development time on complex programs considerably.

Design (1) This is the part of the **classic system life cycle** where the **analyst** shows how the problems identified in the **analysis** phase are to be tackled. More detailed **system flowcharts** and **hierarchical diagrams** may be needed, and more details about the possible ways in which the problems will be solved are covered. This might include **pseudocode algorithms** and detailed design of the **user interface** (**HCI**). The design phase needs to be completed in some detail before the system can be implemented, but **prototypes** may be constructed at this stage to help **clients** choose between alternative systems.

Design (2) This is the part of your **A2 project** where you modularise the problem, identify suitable **algorithms** (not detailed at this stage), identify **data requirements**, suitable **storage media**, produce the **user interface**, design the structures of any **files**, produce **ER diagrams** and/or **flowcharts** if necessary, sort out **data security** and **data integrity** measures and devise an overall **test strategy**.

Desktop publishing This is an **application package** designed specifically for the *precise creation and layout of complex documents* of the sort found in glossy magazines, catalogues and brochures, where complete control over the layout and look of the document is required. It is usual to make use of a conventional **word processor** for the production of the text, and to use a DTP system for *the final page mark up*. A good desktop publishing program usually has the necessary sophistication to control professional typesetting equipment used for large quantity high quality production.

Destination The *place where the data or answer may be stored*. This is typically used when considering **operands** in an **assembly language** instruction.

Determinant This is a term used when designing a **relational database**. *A determinant is an* **attribute**, *(or combination of attributes) which is (are)* **functionally dependent** *on any other attribute (or combination of attributes)*. A 'stock number' and 'item description' is a good example of functional dependence, because they are essentially modelling the same attribute. The stock number therefore *determines* the description, and is a determinant.

Device drivers The **software** used to interface particular devices like **graphics cards**, **network cards** or **printers** to the **operating system**. Device drivers usually go by more specific names like 'graphics card drivers' or 'printer drivers'.

DFD See **data flow diagram**.

Dial up connection See **dial up networking**.

Dial up networking A system which uses a *conventional telephone line* to establish a communication link between two computer systems. It is the system commonly used at home to connect to the **Internet** via a **modem** and telephone socket. Dial up networking does *not use a permanent connection*, although a **broadband** dial up connection may be connected for a very long time indeed; days, weeks or even months.

Dictionary attack A dictionary attack may be made on an **encrypted** password under certain circumstances. If, for example, an encrypted password has been obtained by sniffing a **packet** of data from a **network**, and if the method of **encryption** is known, then a computer is used to encrypt lots of possible words, and, together with other information from the stolen packets, checks to see if the **CRCs** are the same. If they are, the 'message is correct', and the password has therefore been guessed correctly. Unencrypted passwords may also be subjected to a dictionary attack by bombarding the system with thousands of possible passwords. Choosing a sensible **password** will avoid this problem.

Digital audio tape This is a 4 mm tape cartridge system which can store up to about 20 Gigabytes of data. It is thus ideal for some **backup** or **archive** purposes.

Digital camera This is a camera in which pictures can be taken *without using film*. Images are usually stored as jpg files on **flash memory** inside the camera, and then downloaded onto **disk** inside the computer for future processing or printing. High quality images are possible if printed out on good quality glossy paper.

Digital certificate This is a combination of your **public key** and **digital signature**. A digital certificate is used for authentication purposes.

Digital linear tape This is a form of tape storage. The capacity is up to about 40 **Gigabytes**, but 'Super DLT' has capacities up to about 110 Gigabytes. It is thus ideal for some **backup** or **archive** purposes.

Digital signal *A signal that consists only of* **binary digits**. Most modern computers can only process digital data, and thus any **analogue signals** will need to be converted into digital form before they can be processed.

Digital signature This is *a technique used to help guarantee that data is actually from the person who claims to have sent it*. It makes use of **public key** and **private key encryption** systems. If you put a digital signature with your e-mail message, then the combination of the public key and digital signature is called a **digital certificate**.

Digital to analogue converter This is an electronic circuit which converts **digital signals** into **analogue signals**. Conversion the other way round is carried out by an **ADC**.

Digital Versatile Disk This is a *double-sided disk* similar in appearance to a **CD-ROM**, but with considerably higher storage capacity. A DVD may hold from about 4.7 **Gigabytes** of data to just over 17 Gigabytes of data depending on the type (how many sides are used and whether a double or single layer is used).

Digital Versatile Disk Recordable The data on this **DVD** can be written *once only*. It holds about 4 **Gigabytes** of data.

Direct access See **random access**.

Direct Access File *This is a* **data file**, *whose* **records** *may be accessed* **randomly** (see **Random Access**

Memory) by means of a **hashing algorithm** or **index**. You do *not* need to work sequentially through all the previous records to get to an item of interest if the file is organised in this way.

Direct addressing This is a term used in **assembly language** programming where *a specific memory location is referred to*, often by using a **label**. An example is 'mov ax, myData'. Here the data from the memory location referred to by the label 'myData', is being moved into the ax register.

Direct data source This is the name given to **data** which is collected for a specific purpose. If you organise interviews to collect data for analysis in one of your own projects then this would be an example of a direct data source.

Direct implementation This is *a common technique for implementing a system in which the new system becomes live at some particular moment in time*. It is sometimes the only option if the system is complex, and all parts of the system depend on all the other parts (see **phased implementation**). If the new system goes wrong the result could be catastrophic. However, extensive testing of the whole system under simulated use should minimise the possibility of this unfortunate scenario happening.

Directives This is a term normally associated with **assembly language**. *A directive is an operation that does not form part of the assembly language program*. Typically an 'End' command might be used to tell the **assembler** to stop **assembling** the assembly language program because there is no more code after this statement.

Directory *This is the name given to a container that can hold further* **subdirectories** *and* **files**. It is also called a **folder**. The purpose of the directory is to provide a **hierarchical** organisation to files stored on **disk**. This enables us to group together files that naturally belong with each other. E.g. the Windows directory should hold the files associated with the Windows **operating system**, or the Program Files directory might have subfolders which hold the files associated with each **application program**. The user will normally create directories into which documents like word processing files might be saved. The hierarchical directory structure enables the user to organise directories in a huge variety of different ways. It also allows the *same* **file names** to be used many times, as long as they are contained within a different directory.

Directory structure See **hierarchical directory structure**.

Disc Secondary storage media like **CD-ROMs**, **CD-RWs** and **DVDs**. Magnetic media usually use the term 'disk' and optical media usually use the term 'disc'. E.g. a floppy disk or a CD-ROM disc.

Disk Secondary storage media like **floppy disks**, **Zip disks**, and **hard disks**. Magnetic media usually use the term 'disk' and optical media usually use the term 'disc'. E.g. a floppy disk or a CD-ROM disc.

Disk defragmenter A **utility** *that may be run to gather together unused memory on the disk which has arisen as a result of deleting old files and replacing them with new ones*. The new files are unlikely to use the space as efficiently as the original ones, because they are of a different size. If a disk becomes too **fragmented**, large files will be inefficiently stored on many different parts of the disk, and the access times will become very slow.

Disk drives These are the magnetic disk drives used as the main **secondary storage** medium.

Disk farm *This is many* **disks** *working together to provide for the enormous storage requirements of some institutions*. Companies often have what's called a **Terabyte** disk farm. This might be many disks working together to store a Terabyte (or many Terabytes) of data.

Disk Operating System Microsoft's Disk **Operating System** (DOS) is a **command line operating system**. Commands like 'C:' or 'DIR' are typed by the user to interface with the computer. These commands are then processed by the **command line interpreter. Command-driven operating systems** like DOS should be contrasted with **GUI** operating systems like **Windows** and **MacOS**.

Distributed file system This is a system where **files** being processed are obtained from a wide variety of different places like **file servers**, which may be connected via a **LAN** or a **WAN**. Most **client-server** based **networks** operate in this mode. The **Domain Name Server** system is a good example of a distributed file system.

Distributed processing This is the process whereby a particular 'application' can use more than one computer to help complete one or more tasks. Typically a number of computers within an organisation might use networked computers to co-operate on the same task. The SETI (Search for Extra Terrestrial Intelligence) is a good example of this, where thousands of computers around the world are engaged on a small part of the same task, the results of which are then passed back, correlated and processed at SETI headquarters at Berkeley University in the United States.

DLL See **Dynamically linked library**.

DLT See **Digital linear tape**.

DML See **Data manipulation language**.

DNS See **Domain Name System**.

Documentation (1) There are the documents that accompany a computer project, like **technical documentation** and **user documentation**.

Documentation (2) This is *the manual(s) (in paper based or electronic form) which accompany a system*. It may consist of a selection from **user documentation** and **technical documentation**. There may well be an **installation manual**, a **training manual** an **operations manual** and others too.

Domain (1) *This is a term used for organising the* **Internet**. It denotes the top level of an Internet **domain name**. In this context a domain would refer to the '.com' or '.uk', part of the **URL** which is the highest level of the Internet domain name.

Domain (2) On a **LAN** this is a way of dividing up networks into *single administrative units*, under the control of a particular security **database**. Very large organisations might have *different domains* for controlling networked computers for *different departments*. As an example, at a particular university, all computers might be connected to the same **network**, but there might be a 'mechanical engineering department' domain, a 'computer science department' domain and an 'electronic engineering department' domain.

Domain controller A **file server** on a **network** (Microsoft Windows NT, 2000 or XP Professional) that holds *administrative information* like users' accounts and **passwords** etc.

Domain name This is the name given to a **server** (or possibly more than one) on the **Internet** or on a **LAN**. On the **Internet** each **Internet domain name** is a category for registration (see **Internet registrars**) of **web sites** belonging to a particular organisation or individual, and refers to the address (**URL**) of a web site. See **Domain Name System**.

Domain Name Server A **DNS** server is a **file server** on the **Internet** *which holds a database of domain names enabling translation of* **domain names** *into* **IP addresses**. The domain name server system is a very good example of a **distributed file system**, because lots of domain name servers are constantly translating requests for millions of users each day. Without the domain name servers the Internet would rapidly grind to a halt. A domain name server is sometimes called a secondary domain name server to distinguish it from a **primary domain name server**, but both have identical functionality.

Domain Name Service See **Domain Name System**.

Domain Name System This is also called a **Domain Name Service**. It is the system that resolves **domain names** (like www.mywebsite.com) into **IP addresses** like 107.64.21.58, which are then used for **routing** information to find a particular **web site** or other resource on the **Internet**. **Name servers** hold the **databases** that contain all the *current sites* officially registered by the **Internet registrars**, and these are updated quite frequently from the master information held by a limited number of **root servers**. The root servers are usually updated each day by companies which hold the definitive listings for each top level **domain** like '.com', or '.uk' for example.

Domain Name System Server See **Domain Name Server**.

DOS See **Disk Operating System**.

Dot-matrix printer A **printer** that uses *pins which impact on paper through a ribbon*. These tend to be used for invoices in a shop or for printing out stock lists in supermarkets on **fan-fold paper**. These printers are sometimes used with stock lists to create tear-off carbon copies when special paper is used.

DQL See **Data query language**.

DRAM See **Dynamic Random Access Memory**.

Drivers This is the name given to the **software** *that interfaces a particular* **hardware** *device to the* **operating system**. Without a huge variety of drivers you would need a different operating system for each hardware configuration! Examples of drivers would be **graphics card** drivers, **Network Interface Card** drivers, **sound card** drivers and **hard disk** drivers. These are also known as device drivers.

Drum plotter This is a plotter where the pen moves backwards and forwards while a drum (containing the paper) rotates. It can produce large output drawings (A2 and A1) with a minimum or floor space, compared to a **flatbed plotter**.

Dry run This means *manually working through some program code* to try to find an error. It is usual to do this with a pencil and paper, having a table, in which the values of the **constants** and **variables** at any moment in time are written down. Although tedious to do, working through the dry run process will often find a flaw in the logic of your **algorithm** or **program**.

DVD See **Digital Versatile Disc**.

DVD-R See **Digital Versatile Disc Recordable**.

DVD+R A format similar to **DVD-R**. Data can be *recorded once only*.

DVD-RW This is a *rewritable* form of **DVD**. It can store about 4.7 Gigabytes of data. There are other similar systems in operation like **DVD-R**. These discs are ideal for some **backup** and **archive** purposes.

DVD+RW A format similar to **DVD-RW**. Data can be *recorded many times*.

Dynamically linked library This is a routine which may be called up at run time, usually by some **application** that needs it. Different applications may use the same DLLs, and this therefore saves the same routines having to be compiled along with a particular application program. This is sometimes referred to as a dynamic link library. (See **library**.)

Dynamic Random Access Memory This is the standard form of **RAM** that needs to be *constantly refreshed* to maintain its contents. This is *the* most popular form of RAM, and is also known as **DRAM**. All RAM is **volatile**, which means that when the power is removed from the system the data is lost. **CMOS RAM** keeps its power by utilising a small battery.

EAR diagram See **Entity attribute relationship diagram**.

EBCDIC The **Extended Binary Coded Decimal Interchange Code**.

EDI See **Electronic Data Interchange**.

Editor A simple **application program** that is used to create text-based material for editing programs or making changes to files. It is much less sophisticated than a **word processor**, but some will often have special functions like searching for and replacing **control-code** sequences. A good example of a simple text editor is Microsoft's Notepad, but this does not have many special features.

EEPROM This is a **ROM** chip that can be *programmed and erased electrically*, by placing the chip into a special machine. It is useful for programming chips in which the code for a particular system is being developed and tested. The alternative is to program a ROM, but this is permanent, and can only be done by the manufacturer of the chip at the time of manufacture. See **EPROM**.

Electronic Data Interchange This is a form of exchanging electronic documentation between a business and its partners. An agreed format is established for orders and invoices, for example, which can then be processed and sent back to the original company. **EDI** is used extensively by the examination boards, including the AQA. Electronic documents are sent to the participating schools, which then fill in information such as 'predicted grades' and 'coursework marks'. The completed EDI documents are then sent back to the boards, which saves teachers filling in the older style paper-based copies. In this example the school is the Examination Board's business partner.

Electronic memory This is memory where **binary digits** are stored electronically inside a semiconductor chip. The main type of electronic memory is **RAM**, although data may be stored in other electronic chips like **ROM**, or **flash memory**.

Electronic token See **token**.

E-mail Electronic Mail – This is exchanging text and/or other computer-based information and **attachments** via a **communications network** such as the **Internet** or a **LAN**. E-mails are sent to a computerised **mailbox** stored on the **mail server**, which hosts the recipient's mail account. E-mail has now become so popular that many people use it as their main form of communication.

E-mail attachment A **file** that is appended to an **e-mail** message. All forms of **text files** and **binary files** (pictures, sound, videos, word processor documents, spreadsheets etc.) can be sent over the **Internet** making use of this method if **MIME encoding** is used.

Embedded system A system in which *the program to control a device or plant (equipment) like that found in the process control industry is embedded into the device or system*. Small embedded systems are typical of the **hardware** and **software** that is embedded into and controls 'digital cameras', 'mobile phones' and 'games consoles', for example. An example of a larger embedded system would be the system controlling robots that manufacture cars in a car factory.

Encapsulation Encapsulation is a concept used in **object-oriented programming**, whereby *both data* and *methods* are combined into one single mechanism. An important point about encapsulation is that we are able to *hide the internal workings* from other parts of the program that don't need to access them. This means that programmers can't easily mess up work that has already been completed, or mess up work carried out by other programmers working on the same project. Development time is therefore faster because routines are less likely to go wrong when future modifications may be undertaken.

Encoding This is changing data from one form into another. E.g. changing characters into **ASCII** or **Unicode**, or changing pure **binary numbers** into **BCD**. The term is often applied to changing data from **human-readable** form into a form that can be used more easily by a computer.

Encryption This is the process of **encoding** data so that it's difficult or near impossible to decipher by non-authorised persons. The **Public key** and **Private key** encryption systems are now quite common, and **strong encryption** provides the best protection.

End pointer This is a *number* (**vector**) *used to point to the end of a* **data structure** *like a* **FIFO structure**, for example. An end pointer, usually pointing to the end of a list, is represented on a diagram as a number, and an arrow which points to the particular location which contains the last data element in the list.

Entity This is *the term used to describe what a* **relational database table** *is modelling*. E.g. the 'books table' in a library database would be modelling the entity 'books'. *Each relational database table should model one entity only.*

Entity attribute relationship diagram This is an **ER diagram** on which *the* **attributes** *belonging to the* **entities** *have been added.*

EPROM This is a **ROM** chip with a little glass window in the top. An EPROM is programmed electronically, but erased by being placed in a special box and flooding the window with ultraviolet light. It is useful for programming chips in which the code for a particular system is being developed and tested. The alternative is to program a **ROM**, but this is permanent, and can only be done by the manufacturer of the chip at the time of manufacture. See also **EEPROM**.

ER diagram This is an **Entity relationship** diagram. A diagram which pictorially relates various **entities** and the **relationships** that exist between them. Sometimes **attributes** are also included, producing an **EAR diagram**.

Erroneous data This term is used as part of your **A2 project** when dealing with **test data**. This data should be used during the **system testing** phase when *data not expected to work with the system is used for testing purposes*. Appropriate **error messages** should be displayed when this type of data is tested, or the system should reject erroneous data automatically. This term should be compared with **normal data** and **extreme data**.

Error detection In a transmission system, this is *checking to see if any errors have occurred* which may compromise data **integrity**. **Parity**, **checksums** and **CRCs** are various ways of carrying this out in practice.

Error message These are messages designed to assist the user to find the likely source of an error when they are using a computer **program**. These messages should form a vital part of your **user documentation** when carrying out your **A2 project**.

Ethernet A popular system used for **Local Area Networks**. It is a **baseband** system which senses when a **network** is not busy, and then transmits the information. If the network is busy, or if a **collision** occurs (two computers attempting simultaneous communication), then a short (random) period of time is taken before trying again. There are various incarnations of Ethernet, and most types of **PC** have **NICs** that support Ethernet. It is an **asynchronous** transmission system supporting bandwidths of 10 Mbit/sec, 100 Mbit/sec and 1 Gigabit/sec depending on type. 10 Gigabit Ethernet is also available.

Ethernet switch A **switch** *which connects two computers* (or **segments**) *together on an* **Ethernet network**. It is much more efficient than a **hub** because *the full bandwidth is available to the computers being connected*.

Ethics This is *the science of moral order*. It is a philosophical study of how morality affects peoples' behaviour. It is thus the theory of moral values or moral philosophy, or what the moral order ought to be. Computer Scientists, Doctors, Engineers and many other professions have ethical obligations to make sure that the work they are doing does not contravene the rules governing their profession. This term should be compared with **morality**.

Evaluation This is the stage of a computer project when you *compare* the *final system* with the *original* **specification** to see if the project is working effectively and has met the original expectations. It is also useful to constructively criticise the project, and comment, with the benefit of hindsight, what could have been done more effectively. It is part of the **classic system life cycle**.

Even parity This is a method of checking **data integrity**. When using even parity the number of 1s in the data to be transmitted are counted. If there are an odd number of 1s, then the **parity bit** is made equal to '1' to make the total number of '1's even. When the data is received, a new count is made on the number of 1s present, and if it is even, then the data is assumed to be correct. See also **odd parity**.

Event *A* **process** *will run until an event (often created by the user) causes it to halt and run a different process*. An event is used in an **event-driven programming** environment. Modern **operating systems** are event driven, which means that they are constantly responding to events such as 'a mouse click', a 'key being pressed on the keyboard' or 'data being sent out to the printer', for example.

Event-driven program A *program written to respond to* **events** when the program is being run. Most modern **operating systems** and many languages support this mode of operation. Before event driven programs were developed a user could only run one program which took over the entire machine. Event driven systems enable the user to *appear* to do many things at once, like 'surf the net' while 'printing out a word processor file' and 'downloading their e-mail', for example.

Exclusive lock This is a **database** term which occurs when *a record is locked out because it is already in the process of being updated* (or potentially updated) by a different user.

Executable file A **file** that will run on a computer *without* the **compiler** or **interpreter** that was used to create it being present. An executable file is also called an exe file (.exe file).

Execute (1) *Carrying out the operation required* by a particular **machine code** or **assembly language** instruction.

Execute (2) The *act of running a* **computer program** – e.g. executing the program.

Expert system This is a computer system set up to be able to *carry out the function of a human expert* in a particular field like 'oil exploration', 'medical diagnostics' or 'route planning', for example. The expert system has a **knowledge base** of facts set up in a **database**, and is therefore able to answer questions in its particular field of expertise. **Declarative languages** like **Prolog** are ideal for programming these systems. When the knowledge of experts is fed into such a system the process is known as 'mind mining'.

Expert system shell This consists of **software** to help build up a **knowledge base** by using a suitable **interface**, and an **inference engine**. It is typically programmed using **fifth-generation programming language** like **Prolog**.

Exponent This is an **integer** number which is used to modify the **mantissa** in a **floating point** number. If this number is positive, then the **binary point** in the mantissa moves right, or if this number is negative, the binary point moves left. The exponent enables computers to handle very large or very small numbers. *You should note that the exponent is acting as a power of 2.*

Extended ASCII The **ASCII** code uses only *7 bits* for representing characters, because the 8th bit was originally used for **parity checking** purposes. However, other characters, like 'smiley faces' and 'foreign language characters' *could be introduced if the parity bit is not used* for parity checking purposes. If this is done, you can represent 256 characters instead of the original 128 (including all the non-printable ones), and the result is known as the extended ASCII **character set**.

Extended Binary Coded Decimal Interchange Code A system *developed by IBM* for use in their **minicomputer** and **mainframe** computer systems, which is *still in use today*. **Bar code scanners** also make use of ASCII or EBCDIC. EBCDIC should be compared with systems like **ASCII, Extended ASCII** and **Unicode**, used on most **PCs**.

Extreme data This term is used as part of your **A2 project** when dealing with **test data**. This data should be used during the **system testing** phase when *data just within the maximum limits of the system is used*. As an example, a temperature processed by a program might be −273 Celsius (absolute zero), or the upper limit of a **floating point** number used in a program might be 1.235465×10^{87}. This term should be compared with **normal data** and **erroneous data**. See also **boundary data**.

Fact This is a term used in **logic programming**. It helps the programmer to express *something that is unconditionally true*. A fact consists of a **predicate** and a number of **arguments** (which could be zero). Examples of facts from the **Prolog language** are 'female(julie).', which expresses the fact that Julie is a female (one argument) or 'father(james, ray).' which expresses the fact that James is the father of Ray (two arguments). An example of a fact with zero arguments is 'hot.' Each fact in Prolog must be terminated with a full stop, and the programmer must make sure that the order in which the **arguments** occur is consistent.

Factorial The factorial of a number N is worked out using $N \times (N - 1) \times (N - 2) \times \cdots \times 3 \times 2 \times 1$. 5 factorial is therefore $5 \times 4 \times 3 \times 2 \times 1 = 120$. Factorial N is written as N! and 0! by definition is 1. Factorials are used as a classic example of the difference between a **recursive routine** and a *non-recursive routine* to evaluate these numbers.

Fan-fold paper This is **continuous stationery**, (also called continuous forms) in which the paper is driven through the printer by sprockets inserted into the holes at the sides of the page. Fan-fold paper is ideal for the production of stock listings in places like large warehouses, department stores and garages. Fan-fold paper is also used where carbon copies of the printout are made automatically by pins on the **dot-matrix printer** making imprints through the top sheets. This makes it ideal for giving printouts of stock lists to several different departments.

Fat client A conventional **PC** connected to a computer **network** is called a fat client. **Applications** may be delivered from either a local **disk** or a **file server**, and the **operating system** is stored on the local machine. Data may also be stored on a file server or local **hard disks**. Being a conventional PC, a fat client can have a large amount of local processing power, dictated by the **micro processor**/s, the amount of **RAM** and **graphics cards** etc.

Father file This is a second generation **file**, created during the process of serially updating the **son file** with the latest **transaction file**. Three generations of file are usually kept, being the **grandfather**, **father** and **son** files. This provides additional data security in the event of errors being subsequently discovered.

FDM See **frequency division multiplexing**.

Feasibility study A study, carried out by a **systems analyst**, to *see if a problem is suitable for computerisation*. A feasibility study would usually consist of activities like **problem definition**, **problem investigation**, 'alternative solutions' and the 'cost effectiveness or otherwise' of the potential solution. It may be that the conclusion of the feasibility study is that the problem is *not* suitable for solution by a computer, in which case a lot of money would be saved by *not* attempting to build the system.

Fetch The act of *fetching a* **machine code instruction** *from* **main memory** *and putting it into the* **Current Instruction Register** *inside the* **microprocessor**. It is part of the **fetch-decode-execute** (or fetch-execute) cycle.

Fetch-decode-execute cycle This is also known as the **fetch-execute cycle**. This is the cycle, *constantly being carried out by a* **microprocessor**, which fetches **machine code** instructions from **main memory**, decodes these instructions, and then carries out the required actions (execution of the instruction).

Fetch-execute cycle See **fetch-decode-execute cycle**.

Fibre optics A cable in which *plastic* or *glass* is used *instead of copper*. This media makes use of light instead of electricity to transmit the signals. Fibre optic connections are common in computer networks, especially when transmitting at speeds of 1 Gigabit/sec and beyond. Fibre is the preferred medium for **Internet backbone** connections. Unlike copper based cables carrying electricity, optical fibres suffer from very little interference, and no electromagnetic radiation is present which can be used by **hackers** for extracting data from the system.

Field This is a subdivision of a **record**, and corresponds to a single piece of information (an **attribute**) belonging to a record. It also represents a column in a **database table**. Typical examples of fields would be 'Title', 'Author' and 'Publisher' in a library database.

FIFO A First-In-First-Out **data structure** in which the first data item entered is the first data item to be processed. It is the same as a **queue** or **linear queue**. The ideas are the same in principle to the queues found in a shop.

Fifth-generation programming language These *languages are based on* **logic programming**, and *are useful in building up a* **knowledge base** *which can be queried* to see if **facts**, contained within the knowledge base, are 'true' or 'false'. A typical example of a fifth-generation language is **Prolog**. Fifth generation languages are suitable for 'natural language analysis', and other systems which are more convenient to program using a knowledge base instead of a set of **imperative** or **procedural programming** methods.

File A file is a basic unit for the storage of **data**. The string of **bytes** that make up a file can be in a variety of different forms, depending on the data contained within the file. Typical examples are **program files**, **text files**, **graphics files** or various combinations of these and many other things. A **data file** is a special type of file that is split up into **records** and **fields**, and is used by **data-processing** programs and/or **databases**. The file is the unit of storage which presents the related information as a single **entity**, and enables the computer user to store, process, retrieve or use the file in well-defined ways.

File manager This is the part of the **operating system** that manages **files**, either stored on a **peripheral** such as **disk** or **tape**, or stored in the computer's **RAM**. The file manager typically makes sure that no errors occur during a loading or saving process, allocates the amount of RAM needed to load the file into memory, determines the place in the **memory map** where the file will be temporarily stored, or checks that there is sufficient disk space left when a file needs to be saved.

File name This is the name given to a **file**, but not all characters can be used to build up the name because some are reserved for special purposes. Typical examples of illegal characters for the **Windows operating system** are the ':', '*' and '?' characters. It is usual to have a secondary filename extension, which describes the type of file or the application that created it. See **binary files**, **text files**, **program files** and **files**.

File organisation This is the name given to the ways in which files may be organised to help retrieve data in more efficient ways. Typically a **file** may be organised into **serial access**, **sequential access**, **direct access** (**random access**) or indexed sequential access.

File server The name given to a computer on a **network** which is used as *a central resource for storing* **files** *and* **applications** that are available to the **workstations** connected to the network.

File size This is the size of a **file**, in **bytes**. For a simple **file structure** you would typically multiply the number or bytes in each **record** by the number of records in the file to calculate the file size. In practice it is likely to be slightly larger than this because of extra information stored along with the file, which helps to identify the file or to access the **data** contained within it.

File structure A file is a **data structure**, and the term file structure relates to the way that a specific file might be modelled. It could, for example, be a continuous stream of **bytes**, or it may be built up as a collection of **records** which are organised in specific ways (see **file organisation**). Calculation of the **file size** may be achieved from knowledge of the file structure.

File Transfer Protocol One of the **protocols** used on the **Internet** *to transfer large files quickly*. It gets over the limits that some **ISPs** put on file transfers when using **e-mail attachments**. However, the **file server** to which you are connecting must have been set up to support this protocol.

Fingerprint reader *A device which recognises fingerprints that have been previously input to the system*. It is ideal for purposes such as logging on (without the need for, or in addition to **passwords**) or for checking identities in libraries etc. This saves the need to carry around an ID card. Several fingerprints may be entered, just in case you cut your finger and have a plaster on the one you would normally use. Finger print readers have come down in price and are now very cost effective, even for small schools or offices.

Firewall This is usually **hardware** or **software**, *set up to provide additional security (against* **hackers***) between a* **LAN** *and the* **Internet** (via a **proxy server** acting as a **gateway**) *or a* **client machine** *and the Internet*. A firewall thus helps to prevent unauthorised access to machines, either locally or on a **network**. It does this by obeying a set of default rules, or other rules that have been added to protect a particular organisation. Typically these may include filtering **packets**, blocking **ports** and special security measures for systems using a **VPN**, **telnet** or the **ftp protocol** for example.

First-generation language The first generation of computer programming language is **machine code**. It is very tedious and error prone to use because it consists solely of **binary digits**.

First normal form This is one of the rules carried out to ensure errors are minimised when designing a **relational database**. This rule states that **attributes** *having multiple values (repeating values) must be removed so that the rows* (**records**) *in a* **table** *are all of the same length*. You should remember that a number of conditions *must* be satisfied before first normal form can be applied. Typical of these conditions are '**tables** must have a unique **primary key**', 'a table should model one **entity** only' and 'all attribute names must be different'. See also **second normal form**, **third normal form** and **BCNF**.

Fixed length record *All the* **records** *within a* **data file** *are of a fixed length*. This leads to more efficient **algorithms** for accessing the **data** contained within the record very quickly, but is often wasteful of storage space, as the length of record has to be able to accommodate the longest known entry, or very long entries may have to be cut off.

Fixed partitioning **Memory** *is allocated to programs and* **tasks** (**applications**) *in fixed sized chunks*. This is easier to manage compared to **variable partitioning**, but some memory will be wasted. All the fixed partitions do *not* have to be of the same size.

Fixed point number In practice *all numbers are represented in a fixed register length*, which leads to a limitation of the range of numbers that can be represented. There are two types of fixed-point number representation, **integer fixed point** and **fractional fixed point**, which are simply examples of fixed point. This method thus gives the greatest precision, and should be compared with a **floating point number**.

Flag *A flag is used for indicating the status of something*. Examples could be 'flagging the user's attention to some error that might have occurred' or to 'set the carry flag inside a microprocessor indicating that an **arithmetic overflow** has occurred' (i.e. the number is too big to be stored in the available space). The actual mechanisms for using a flag could include 'setting a bit in a **register**' when using **assembly language**, or 'setting a **Boolean** variable in a program to true or false' when using a **high-level language**.

Flag register A **special purpose register** in which **bits** *are assigned to monitor the states of various operations like* '**arithmetic overflow**', 'whether a **carry** has occurred' or 'whether an **interrupt** has occurred' etc. The **assembly language** programmer would use the state of these **flags** as a basis for decision making in the program.

Flash memory *A* **ROM** *that can be programmed and reprogrammed in situ* (i.e. inside the computer). It has become popular because computers in which the **BIOS** is stored in flash memory can have the **ROM BIOS** upgraded without having to physically remove the old ROM chips from the **motherboard** and replace them with new ones. This is also the type of memory used inside digital still or digital video cameras. It is the same as **flash ROM**. *These devices are being used increasingly to transfer data between computers and other devices* such as digital cameras.

Flash ROM See **flash memory**.

Flat file database This is a database in which a single **table** or **file** is used to store all the **records**. This should be compared with a **relational database**, which normally consists of a number of related tables.

Flatbed plotter See **plotter**.

Floating point This representation of a **binary number** has a structure *which is split into two parts, called the* **mantissa** *and the* **exponent**. The mantissa represents a **fractional fixed point binary number** and the exponent holds a **two's complement integer** binary number which is used to determine the final position of the **binary point**. This number format is the binary equivalent of decimal numbers written using scientific notation or standard form like 2.34×10^{13}, for example. Here 2.34 is the mantissa and 13 is the exponent.

Floppy disk A 3.5 inch **disk** which can store about 1.44 **Mbyte** of data. It is also called a floppy. This is still a very cheap method of getting data from one computer to another, but the storage capacity is limited and the reliability is low. A floppy disk rotates at about 300 r.p.m., which is very slow compared to rotation speeds in excess of 15,000 r.p.m. for fast **hard disks**. It is thus very slow to access the data, which is usually a few fractions of a second, compared to hard disk access times of just a few msec or less. You should *never* rely on a floppy disk as your only source of **backup** for any important files.

Flowchart This is the general name for a **program flowchart** or a **system flowchart**. It is also possible to use the program flowchart symbols to express more general **algorithms** from 'crossing the road' to 'sorting a list of numbers into ascending order'.

Flowgraph A graphing system consisting of nodes and arcs which, for the purposes of A2 Computing, are used to help determine the possible paths through the program code when carrying out **white box testing**.

Folder See **directory**.

Footer (1) This is a term used to describe the place at the bottom of a document which holds information like page number, logo or date. However, virtually any information (graphics too) can be inserted in the footer. See also **header**.

Footer (2) See **end pointer**.

Foreign key field This is a term used when dealing with a **relational database**. A foreign key is a field in one table which is a **primary key field** (or secondary key field) in another table, thus creating a link between the two tables in a relational database.

Form (1) This is *the name given to the record-card system* typically used when creating a **database**. It is far easier for users to view the data via a form, than to make use of the alternative tabular view of the data. **Tables** and forms are used extensively in databases like Microsoft Access.

Form (2) A page on a **web site** into which users may type information. When using forms this creates a dynamic web site in which information typed in by the users may be captured and stored in a **database** on a **file server**.

Formal language A *computer-based language* like **C++** or **Visual Basic**. This should be compared to a **natural language**, like English or Spanish. A formal language is *not context sensitive*, and obeys strict rules of **syntax**.

FORTRAN FORmula TRANslator or FORmula TRANslation. A **high-level language** *ideally suited for mathematics, engineering and science*. This is one of the languages used by the Meteorological Office to help forecast the weather. FORTRAN has been around for many years and is still used extensively.

Fourth-generation language This is *the next generation after the* **procedural programming** *languages*. Typical examples include **macro** languages like Microsoft's **VBA**, and **SQL** languages as used on **database servers**. These are higher-level languages because commands like 'Sort' would be used instead of writing the **imperative** elements to actually carry out the details of the sorting process. A fourth generation language is yet further removed from what actually happens inside the machine.

Fractional binary number This is a **binary number** with a fractional part e.g. the number 1.01 would be a fractional binary number that represents 1.25 decimal. The **binary point** separates the **integer** and fractional parts of the binary number. See also **arithmetic underflow**.

Fractional fixed point This representation of a **binary number** uses a **register** in which *the position of the* **binary point** *is fixed and is assumed to be in-*

between the first and second **most significant bits**. The register is not able to hold any **integer fixed point numbers**, and the range depends upon the number of bits being used for the register. An 8-bit fractional fixed point register may be used to represent the following numbers. The maximum positive is 1 – ^{7} and the minimum positive is ^{7}. The maximum negative is –1 and minimum negative is – ^{7}. Integer fixed point and fractional fixed point are simply different examples of **fixed point numbers**. See also **floating point**.

Fragmented A term used when a **disk** or **RAM** *becomes slow to respond and inefficient because of the 'holes' left behind by dynamic allocation of files saved to disk, or, in the case of RAM,* **memory management** *by the technique of* **variable partitioning**. To get over this problem a utility is run on a disk called a **disk defragmenter**, or the **operating system** will suspend tasks being run while it gathers up all of the unused memory and joins them together to form a more usable contiguous space which can then be reallocated to other **tasks**.

Free memory pointer The name given to a **pointer** (*number* or **vector**) which *points to the next item of free memory in a list of data*. Such pointers are useful for helping to implement **linked list data structures**, and the free memory pointer helps to manage the available **nodes** in the data structure that don't currently contain any valid data. If data gets deleted from a linked list the free memory pointers are updated to reflect the node which can now be used to store some other data.

Freedom of Information Act This act gives individuals two different rights. The first *is the right to be told if information is being held about them*, and the second is *the right to be able to see this information*. However, there may be some restrictions imposed on this. See also **Data Protection Act**.

Frequency division multiplexing This is a method of *sending different signals over the same communications link in which different data signals are modulated onto different* **carrier signals** making *use of different frequencies*. Simultaneous transmission of different signals can be achieved by using this method.

FROM This is a term associated with a **relational database** when defining a **query**. The **key word** 'FROM' is used to identify the **table** name *from* which data will be retrieved when using **SQL**.

FTP See **File Transfer Protocol**.

Full duplex A method of communication in which *signals may be transmitted in both directions simultaneously* (e.g. the telephone or a two-way radio system).

Function In programming, this is *the name given to a* **subprogram** *which is called by name, and returns a single value result*. If, for example, we use the 'square root' function, then in a particular **high-level programming language** this may be called by the **program statement** 'x = SQRT(4)', which would return a single value of x = 2. Most programming languages also allow users to define their own functions, and mathematically based high-level languages like **FORTRAN** will even return the complex root too.

Functional dependence When designing a **relational database**, *a functional dependence is a unique association* between two **attributes**. A good example of this would be 'item number' and 'item description' in a stock database. There is a unique association between these attributes because they describe the same thing.

Functional programming This **paradigm** *defines what has to be done by solving a problem as though it were written as a series of mathematical or other functions*. Functions rather than sequences of commands (**imperatives**) typify this language. Examples are Clean, LISP and Haskell. Functional programming languages rely heavily on **recursion**, which can be used to solve complex problems with a minimum amount of cleverly written code.

Games console A special **interface** enabling games to be played more easily on a specialist games machine or computer. Typical of these are Sony's PlayStation and Microsoft's X-Box.

Gateway This device is *usually a computer, placed on a* **network**, *which may connect different types (or the same type) of network together.* Gateways can also carry out **protocol** conversion, and operate at level 4 (**layer 4**) and above on the **ISO OSI seven layer model**. Modern **routers** are taking over the job of some of these gateways.

Gbyte See **Gigabyte**.

General purpose application software This is **software** *for general purposes use like* **word processors, presentation packages, spreadsheets** *and* **databases**. *General purpose software is used by the vast majority of computer users*, and should be compared with **special purpose application software**, which is not.

General purpose register **Registers** may be **general purpose** or **special purpose**. *A general purpose register is a register which can be assigned by the* **assembly language** *programmer for a variety of different tasks.* A register, for example, could be used to implement different **stacks** or be used as a **pointer** for some **data structure** needed for a particular assembly language program.

Generalisation This is a term used in **object-oriented analysis**, and describes one sort of **relationship** which can be shown on a **class diagram**. *An important type of generalisation is used to define* **inheritance**, *where a* **derived class** *would inherit properties from the* **base class** *or parent class.* When using a class diagram, instead of a solid line, *a generalisation is shown by a solid arrow with the head pointing to the parent class.* When modelling generalisations we are trying to establish which classes have the same characteristics in common with those characteristics present in a **superclass**. *Generalisation is just one approach to modelling inheritance.* The other is **specialisation**. See also **object-oriented analysis** and **object analysis diagrams**.

Generations of files See **grandfather file**, **father file** and **son File**.

Gigabyte One Gigabyte = 1024 × 1024 × 1024 = 1,073,741,824 **bytes** of data.

Global variable In programming, a **variable** that is recognised throughout the entire **program**, including inside **subroutines** and **procedures**. Any subroutine or procedure that uses this variable will alter all occurrences of this variable throughout the entire program. Compare with the term **local variable**.

Grandfather file This is a third generation file, (and usually final) created during the process of serially updating the **father file** with the latest **transaction file**. Three generations of file are usually kept, being the **grandfather**, **father** and **son** files. This provides additional data security in the event of errors being subsequently discovered.

Graphical User Interface A **user interface** making use of **windows**, **pointers**, **icons**, **menus** and mice. This type of interface enables users to perform operations like 'drag and drop'. Typical of this type of interface are Microsoft **Windows** and Apple **MacOS**.

Graphics The name given to pictures used on a computer. Pictures are usually one of two types, namely **bit-mapped graphics** or **vector-based graphics**.

Graphics card An electronic circuit board (**daughter board**) plugged in to the main **motherboard** to provide extra power to run complex graphic programs at high resolution and with many colours. There are lots of different types of graphics card, and special **graphics card drivers** are needed to interface each one with a particular **operating system**.

Graphics tablet A device, usually used by artists or engineers, to input data into a **CAD package** or **Art package** by means of a stylus. It is far easier to draw pictures on the computer screen with this device compared to using a conventional mouse. On a good graphics tablet the pen is usually pressure sensitive, and this produces a more natural interface for drawing compared to using a device in which the pressure exerted on the pen or pencil has no effect.

GROUP BY This is a term sometimes used when producing queries in a **relational database**. *GROUP BY is an* **SQL key word** *used to display the result of a* **query** *in some specific order, but on groups instead of an entire column of data.*

Groups This is a term used to describe groups that have been set up by a network administrator to control 'who can do what', mainly in terms of security settings. Therefore one group may be able to run a particular application where another group may not, or one group might be able to see sensitive data and another group may not.

Guaranteed bandwidth A communication system in which a *minimum* **baud rate** *is guaranteed.* Telecommunication companies are able to provide this for the transmission of **real time audio**, **real time video** and **real time voice** data using **networks** like **ATM**.

GUI See **Graphical User Interface**.

Hackers These are the people who carry out **hacking**.

Hacking The *unauthorised* use of a computer. Hacking is carried out by **hackers**, who are people who, for perverse pleasure or financial gain, like illegally breaking the security of systems, especially those run by large multinational institutions and government agencies.

Handshaking This is *a method of establishing the readiness to open a communication channel between two different devices*. At a simple level, the transmitting device might check to see if the receiving device is ready, like the methods used when a computer is ready to print a page to the printer. More complex handshaking could establish information like the **baud rate** and **error checking** methods to be used, like the methods used when one **modem** communicates with another.

Hard copy The output from a **printer**, i.e. *a paper-based copy*. This should be contrasted with **soft copy**.

Hard disk A (usually) fixed **disk** fitted inside a computer system and used as the main **secondary storage** device. The capacity is measured in **bytes** and the speed is measured in bytes transferred per second into the computer system. The price of hard disks seems to go down in ever increasing spirals while the storage capacity of hard disks seems to go up at an amazing rate. A hard disk is a very reliable form of storage and is ideal for important **backups**.

Hardware *All the physical computer equipment* like **motherboards**, **disk drives**, **keyboards**, **disks**, **printers** and **mice** etc.

Hash table A table or an **array**, usually arranged in some particular order produced by a **hashing function**. A hash table would normally store **pointers** which point to where the actual data to be accessed is stored.

Hash total This is *a special number calculated from data* which is to be transmitted or processed in some way. *It acts as an error-checking mechanism* for checking the **integrity** of the transmitted or processed data. A hash total is calculated by using some suitable **hashing algorithm**, and is then added to the data to be transmitted. At the other end of the transmission, after the data has been received, the hash total is recalculated using the same hashing algorithm. If the two hash totals are the same, then the data is assumed not to be corrupt. If the numbers are different, then the data has been corrupted and must be transmitted again. This system is also useful to determine if a document or **file** has been tampered with in some way, and is also used for **digital signatures**.

Hashing *This is a method for finding stored data items very quickly*. Key information, like customer ID or surname, for example, is fed into a **hashing function**, which is a mathematical way of generating some numeric code that points to a **hash table** containing the actual **address** (or position within a **file**) at which the real data is stored. Using **modulo arithmetic**, hashing functions can also ensure that the data to be stored fits within a well-defined range of locations, and a good hashing algorithm should also spread the data evenly over these locations. *Don't confuse the term* **hashing** *or* **hash function** *with* **hash totals**, which are used as a check on the **integrity** of **data**.

Hashing algorithm This is a method used for calculating a **hash total**. It is usual to add together a set of numbers generated from various **fields** within a **file**. You don't have to work these out for yourself, as special programs will provide a total for you.

Hashing function See **hashing algorithm**.

HCI *This is the Human Computer Interface* – see **user interface**. HCI is also used in the context of Human Computer Interaction.

Head This is the name given to the item at the beginning of a **list** in a language like **Prolog**.

Header (1) This is a term used to describe the place at the top of a document which holds information like page number, logo or date. However, virtually any information (graphics too) can be inserted in the header. Also see **footer**.

Header (2) In a network, the headers contain information added to a **packet** of data. This could contain extra information like the **protocol** being used, and the destination address of the packet, for example.

Header (3) See **start pointer**.

Heap A heap is an area of memory set up for the purposes of temporary storage. Unlike **stacks** or **queues**, the heap is a more random and higgledy-piggledy use of memory, in which blocks of memory are assigned when needed.

Heterogeneous data type This is a **data type** in which data elements may be of different types. Typical of this is a **file** or a **database**, where **attributes** in the file or the **table** will probably be different. An **array** could be used to model these data types if it is split up into smaller arrays in which the data in each array is homogeneous. This should be compared with the term **homogeneous data type**.

Hex See **hexadecimal**.

Hexadecimal A **number base** having *sixteen unique characters* consisting of the set

{0,1,2,3,4,5,6,7,8,9,A,B,C,D,E,F}. Hexadecimal is useful for computers because of the convenient way of representing **binary** numbers in a form more convenient to humans. For example, 8F8B (a number in **hex**) is easier to remember than 1000111110001011, (the same number in binary). Hexadecimal is also used because of the very simple relationship between hex and binary, which enables very simple conversion methods.

Hierarchical data structure A **data structure**, similar in principle to a family tree, in which a hierarchy is implemented from the way in which the data structure is drawn. These hierarchical relationships do not necessarily reflect the importance of any element within the data structure.

Hierarchical diagram A tree type diagram in which the **root** usually represents a problem to be solved, and separate branches from the root show the sub problems. It is likely that each sub problem will also need to be divided up into further tree structures. This type of diagram is ideal for a **top-down analysis** of the problem, and splits the problem into convenient modules, which may be tackled by different people or teams of people if necessary.

Hierarchical directory structure A system, based on **directories**, that resembles a **tree**. The **root directory** is at the top level, and all other directories are subordinate to the root. This **hierarchical data structure** making use of directories enables users to manage and find resources more easily, compared to putting all files within a single container. It also allows the same **file names** to be used many times, as long as they are contained within a different directory.

High-level language This is a computer programming language which is English-like and thus closer to the way that humans think. Compare this with **low-level languages** like **assembly language** and **machine code**, which are closer to the way in which the computer actually operates. Typical examples of high-level languages are **Visual BASIC**, **C++**, **Delphi**, **Pascal**, **FORTRAN** and **Java**.

Hit Successfully locating a data item of interest is called a hit. This term is applied to finding a **record** in a **database** or **file** (see **hit rate**). It is also applied to successfully retrieving a web page from a **web site**, or successfully retrieving an item of data from **cache memory**.

Hit rate This is a term associated with finding an item of data like retrieving a specific piece of data from a **file**, for example. *The hit rate is a measure of the success, or how many accesses have to be done to find the data.* See also **hit**.

Hit rate This is a term associated with finding an item of data like retrieving a specific piece of data from a **file**, for example. *The hit rate is a measure of the success, or how many searches or accesses have to be done to find the data.* A **binary search** should provide a better (lower) hit rate than a **linear search** because, on average, you need less searching to find a particular item. See also **hit**.

Homogeneous data type This is a **data type** in which all data elements must be of the same type. Typical of this is an **array**, where all the elements of the array must be of the same data type, like 'string' or 'numeric', for example. This should be compared with the term **heterogeneous data type**.

Host ID This is the remainder of the **IP address** after the **Network ID** part has been removed. Taking an example for a **class A network**, if the IP address is 101.233.12.55, then the Network ID would be 101, therefore the host ID would be the remainder of the IP address which in this case is 233.12.55. The host ID determines the number of unique computers that may be placed on the network.

HTML See **HyperText Mark-up Language**.

HTML command A command in the **HTML** language like '<H1> Computing Department </H1>', which displays the heading (H1 size) Computer Department at the top of the **browser** window.

HTTP See **HyperText Transfer Protocol**.

HTTPS This is the secure (**encrypted** version) of **HTTP**. 128-bit **encryption** is now common for important financial and other similar **transactions** carried out over the **Internet**. The security is provided by another protocol called SSL or Secure Sockets Layer, which runs underneath the **HTTP protocol**.

Hub *A piece of* **hardware** *into which* **networked** *computers may be plugged, enabling the computers to communicate with each other.* At the simplest level a small box with 4 connections could be used at home to network three or four different computers, and one can thus see that the box forms the hub of the network, with the wires to the computer looking like the spokes on a wheel. In the case of the small box, all computers must share the same **bandwidth**. At a more complex level, many larger **intelligent hubs** are connected together to build up **tree networks** in business or educational institutions. **Managed hubs** enable data to be **routed** more intelligently, so that computers on one sub network (**segment**) do not interfere with computers on a different sub network, unless the data needs to be transmitted from one network to the other.

Human oriented language This is a computer **programming language** which is closer to the way that humans think instead of being closer to the way in which a particular machine operates. Typical of these would be the **high-level languages**. Compare this term with **machine oriented language**.

Human readable This is data that can be read by humans without the aid of a computer. E.g. text on a piece of paper, the **MICR** characters at the bottom of bank cheques or the numbers printed along with a **bar code** on a product.

Hyperlink See **hypertext link**.

Hypertext link This is the method by which *multiple documents may be linked*. When clicked over with the mouse, a hypertext link enables the user to jump to a set position within the same document or some other document. As long as the full path name is available, documents may reside on **web servers** connected to **LANs** and **WANs** in any part of the world.

HyperText Mark-up Language HTML stands for Hypertext Mark-up Language and is used on the **Internet** and **intranets**. It is the **program** code which lies behind the construction of web pages. HTML is called a **page description language** because it is used to describe how a **web page** will be displayed on the user's **web browser**.

HyperText Transfer Protocol This is **HTTP**, one of the main **protocols** used for the distribution of **web pages** on the **Internet** and on **intranets**.

I/O Input/Output. This term is commonly applied to items like **I/O ports**. This is a place through which data can travel into the computer or data can travel from the computer to **peripheral** devices like **keyboards**, **printers** and **mice**, for example.

I/O ports A place where data may be fed into or got out of a computer. Typical examples of I/O ports are the **serial ports**, **USB ports** and **parallel ports**. A variety of devices like **mice**, **keyboards**, **printers** and **digital cameras** may be connected to some of these I/O ports.

IAS See **Immediate Access Store**.

Icons These are the small on-screen pictures representing objects like **disks**, **files**, shortcuts and tools for applications etc. which, when clicked over with a mouse, perform a variety of common operations. Along with **windows**, **menus** and **pointers**, these icons form an integral part of a **GUI operating system**.

Identifier A *string of characters representing the name or label that is given to entities like* **variables**, **constants** and **procedures** etc. The **syntax** rules for a particular programming language would determine if a particular character string can be used for a particular identifier. Spaces, for example, are not usually allowed in variable names, and this limitation is overcome by using names like 'Quantity_In_Stock', for example, where the underscore character replaces a space. Note how the use of the underscore character still maintains the readability of the name of the variable or constant, and this is essential to maintain good **structured programming** style.

Immediate Access Store An *alternative name* for **main memory** or **RAM**.

Immediate addressing This is a term used in **assembly language** programming where *the data appears immediately after the* **operation code**. An example is 'mov, ax, 20'. Here the decimal number 20 is generated immediately and placed into the **destination** register which, in this case, is the ax register.

Imperative programming paradigm The imperative programming paradigm typifies languages like **machine code, assembly language, DML** (a **data manipulation language** from **SQL**) and the very early versions of the **high-level language BASIC**. It involves writing sequences of instructions (called imperatives), which directly control the state of the system. It is up to the programmer to control the system in rudimentary ways, compared to using **procedural programming**.

Implementation This is part of the **classic system life cycle** where programmers and others take the specifications and methods outlined by the analyst in the **analysis** and **design** phases, and get them working by writing **computer program** code or using other **software**. The system has already been modularised, and the implementation is usually a matter of building up and testing each module, before any **integration testing** is carried out.

Independent certification authority This is a company set up to act as a *third party* source for issuing **digital certificates**. Companies like these act *as trusted sources, who guarantee that individuals involved in transactions are who they say they are*. If an individual misuses this trust they are struck off the register.

Index (1) A method of keeping track of where something is stored within a **file** or on **disk**, for example. By using the index entries, the records do not have to be searched sequentially to find an item of interest. See also **indexed sequential file**.

Index (2) In a **relational database** this is the list of numbers that are assigned to the index **fields**, usually used for 'fast searching' or 'sorting' of the records within the database. See also **primary index** and **secondary index**.

Indexed addressing This is a term used in **assembly language** programming *where a number contained in one* **register** *is usually used in combination with a number contained in another register to point to a memory location of interest*. An example is 'mov cx, [bx + di]'. Here the bx and di registers are combined to create an address which is used to point to a memory location from where the data can be obtained. The index register is then incremented to point to the next item of data. Indexed addressing is very useful for setting up **arrays**.

Indexed sequential file See **index (1)**.

Indirect addressing This is a term used in **assembly language** programming where *a number inside a* **register** *or memory location is used to point to a memory location of interest*. An example is 'mov ax, [bx]'. This means the number inside the memory location pointed to by the bx register will be moved into the ax register. Here the square brackets mean that we are pointing to a memory location from where the actual data is to be obtained.

Indirect data source This is the term applied when using data that was originally collected for some other purpose. A typical example of this would be using the results of surveys and statistics gathered from other sources to include in one of your projects.

Inference engine This is software that is used to help build up a **knowledge base** using a high-level programming language like **Prolog**. An inference engine will infer new **facts** by using the inference **rules** which have been programmed into the knowledge base.

Information *After meaning (structure) has been applied to raw* **data** *it becomes information*, i.e. something that has a specific meaning in the context in which it is being used. The numbers 072101108108111 would be meaningless data to most, but told that each triplet is the decimal value for the **ASCII** code, then we decode the numbers to realise the message means 'Hello', and it has now become information. (Assuming, of course, that you can speak English.)

Information collection See **system life cycle**.

Information rate The *rate at which information (symbols like characters or numbers etc.) is transmitted*. This is not usually the same as the **baud rate** or **bit rate**, because of overheads like **start bits** and **stop bits**, **modulation** methods and other checks like **CRCs** for **data integrity**.

Information requirements of a system This term is used when performing a **systems analysis**. The 'information requirements of a system' is basically a list of the things that the new system must do. It is thus a set of objectives which must be achieved if the new computerised system is to be successfully implemented. See **system life cycle**.

Inheritance Inheritance is a useful mechanism used in **object-oriented programming** where *a* **derived class** *can inherit properties from a* **base class**. This mechanism is useful because we can *reuse code which is already tried and tested*. We can selectively inherit some or all of the properties by making use of keywords like **public**, **private** and **protected**. This enables the base class, and thus the programmers who wrote the original code, to control what may or may not be inherited.

Inheritance diagram This type of diagram is useful for helping to undertake an **object-oriented analysis** *before* any **object-oriented programming** is done. **Inheritance** may be shown on a **class diagram**. An inheritance diagram is drawn rather like a **hierarchical diagram** on which the **superclass** is shown at the top inside a square box, and the three-compartment notation (see **class diagram**) used to show the class name, **class attributes** and **class operations** may be included. Each **subclass** is shown on the next level of the diagram, with directed links to the superclass. Other levels might be required depending on the complexity of the model, because other subclasses may inherit properties from those on the second level of the inheritance diagram. As an example, the superclass might be 'People at School' and the subclasses might be 'Students', 'Teachers', 'Administrators', 'Caretakers' and 'Cleaners'. These subclasses all inherit the properties of people (like 'home address', 'telephone number' etc.) but have their own data and information for each subclass too. If you are undertaking an A2 project involving an object-oriented language like **C++**, **Java** or **VisualBasic.NET**, then you should have this type of diagram in the **analysis** section of your project. See also **object-oriented analysis** and **object analysis diagrams**.

Ink jet printer This is a high-quality print system, especially if special (glossy) paper is used. This technology is common in the home, and is used in the office for very low-volume print runs. The printers are usually cost effective to buy, but the cartridges to replenish the ink are usually very expensive. Large format A3 and A2 inkjet printers have replaced similar sized plotters in the engineering industry, but the very large plotters (A2, A1, A0 and larger) have no competition from ink jet printers as yet. **Laser printers** are more suitable for office and high-volume environments.

In-order traversal When **traversing** a **tree structure** using this method we visit **nodes** in the order 'Left', 'Root' and 'Right'. The term *in-order* refers to the fact that we visit the **root node** *in the middle*. If the tree has **subtrees**, we make a **recursive** call to traverse the subtree using the in-order traversal mechanism again.

Input device *Any device designed to get data into a computer system*. Examples would be **keyboards**, **mice**, **graphics tablets**, **scanners** and **MICR**.

Insertion sort This **sorting algorithm** starts with just two numbers from the list of numbers to be sorted. The second number is then placed in the appropriate position (if we are sorting ascending numerical, then the second number gets placed after the first). We then get to the third number from the unsorted list, and this number is *inserted* into the right place so we end up with three numbers correctly sorted. This process goes on, inserting the next numbers in the sorted list until all numbers in the unsorted list have been processed, in which case the entire list is sorted.

Installation manual On larger systems installation might be a complex procedure, and *an installation manual is usually provided to enable* **commissioning engineers** *to set up the system*. Installation of systems in large companies might take days or even weeks, and this manual gives the sequence of operations that must be gone through to commission the system for a customer.

Instance This is a term used in **object-oriented programming**. It is the name given to *the creation of an* **object** *by creating an instance* (a particular instance) *of that* **class**. This is also known as *instantiation*. As an example, there might be a class of 'Teapots' and an instance of this 'Teapot class' might be 'Teapots which are in the shape of a monkey'.

Instruction set *The* set of **machine code** instructions that operate on a particular type of **microprocessor**. *No set of instructions, designed for use on one type of microprocessor will work with any another*, thus ensuring incompatibility between systems that use different microprocessors. Examples of different instruction sets are the Apple Mac and the PC, which make use of the Motorola and Intel (or AMD etc.) microprocessor families respectively. Some

applications, like Microsoft Office, have versions which will allow this **application software** to work on several different **platforms**.

Integer A numeric **data type** *which can take on whole numbers only*. Most programming languages support a variety of integer **variables** depending on the range of numbers used.

Integer fixed point This representation of a **binary number** uses a **register** in which *the position of the* **binary point** *is assumed to be at the end (right-hand side)*. No number less than one can therefore be represented, and the range depends upon the number of bits being used for the **register**. An 8-bit integer fixed point register may be used to represent positive numbers 0 to 255, or, if **two's complement representation** is used, the numbers from −128 to +127 may be represented.

Integrated package This is **software** that usually integrates a simpler **word processor**, **spreadsheet** and **database** etc. into a single package. The package is designed to enable users to transfer information more easily between the different parts of the package. However, each part does not usually have the sophistication of a fully blown **application package** where the word processor, spreadsheet and database would be provided separately. Microsoft Works is a good example of an integrated package, where the functionality would be less than the functionality in the suite of programs called Microsoft Office.

Integration testing *Two or more* **modules** (which have already been **module tested**) *are joined to check that they work properly together*. If a system works well before a particular module has been introduced, then any errors are likely to be with the module just added, or at least with the interaction of the module just added with one of the other modules. It is useful to show the interrelation of each module by using a **hierarchical diagram**. Modules *are usually added one at a time until the complete system is built up and tested in its entirety*.

Integrity See **data integrity**.

Intelligent bridge A **bridge** *which can be programmed to block out or let through data between different* **segments** *on a* **LAN**. It can thus be used for effective management of **bandwidth**, by making sure that traffic, intended for one particular network does not get transmitted to others. Some bridges are capable of learning by observation of the traffic flow, and setting up their own internal systems to maximise the bandwidth of the network, based on experience of what has happened previously. These are also known as learning bridges.

Intelligent hub This is a network hub that may be programmed remotely by a network administrator to enhance functionality like accumulating network statistics, for example. An intelligent hub would have an **IP address**, and therefore do more than an ordinary hub, which simply distributes the signals.

Intelligent switches An **Ethernet switch** with much added functionality. There are *many software modules that can be added to sophisticated switches for a variety of purposes* such as providing statistics about what the switch is doing or blocking certain communication channels, for example. An unintelligent **switch** would only be able to slavishly carry out the communication requests of the system.

Interactive operating system This is a type of **operating system**, like **Windows** or the **MacOS**, which *carries out a constant dialogue with the user, and allows the user to do virtually anything that can be done whenever they want to do it* (i.e. run a word processor, surf the net, play a CD, send an e-mail etc.). This should be compared with a **batch operating system**, which is *not* interactive.

Interactive whiteboard This is a board (like a blackboard used for teaching purposes) which, when used in conjunction with a suitable multimedia **projector**, can display all computer output in the conventional way. In addition to this, a special pen, which interacts with the board (how it does this depends on the type of board) can be used to provide all the functionality of the mouse, or to produce an annotation layer over the conventional computer screen (i.e. the teacher can write over the computer image). In addition to this, the board can be put into a mode where it can be used for conventional 'Chalk and Talk' techniques. This means that a teacher now has a conventional 'black' board, on which the pen appears to write as a piece of chalk. Some advantages of this over a conventional board are having access to hundreds of different screens, or to save and print out the notes just made on the board by the teacher. Lesson notes could also be made available over an **intranet** or the **Internet**.

Interface This is a general term for the interaction or communication at the boundary between the computer and other entities like **users** or **peripherals**. Typical examples are the **user interface**, a **printer** interface or a **USB** interface.

Intermediate byte code This is **Java** *that has been translated into a form that can run on a* **Java virtual machine**. When Java programs are compiled or interpreted, the result is intermediate byte code. Different platforms would have different versions of the Java virtual machine, which translates the intermediate byte code into a form which a particular **platform** will be able to execute.

Internal bus The name given to the bus system inside a **microprocessor** chip.

Internal schema See **physical schema**.

International standards organisation An *international body which is responsible for the creation of standards which are then agreed internationally*, thus ensuring consistency across a range of products and services. This body is made up of a large number of national standards organisations from many different countries.

Internet *A worldwide* **network** of **communication networks** *which use the* **TCP/IP protocol** *for communication purposes*. Users can be linked to the Internet via a **dial up connection**, a **leased line** connection or via a **proxy server** connecting the users on a **LAN**. Millions of **host computers** serve a variety of information to hundreds of different countries. Technically, if a capital 'I' is used for 'Internet', then this refers to the worldwide network we all know, but if a small 'i' is used then it simply refers to a 'network of other networks', of which the Internet is the biggest example. However, the terms 'internet' and 'Internet' are commonly used to mean one and the same thing, especially in non-technical articles such as those found in some parts of the press.

Internet backbone These are the fast national and international high-**bandwidth** connections which carry huge amounts of **Internet** traffic. Typically these might link cities together, but the term backbone is also used in a **LAN** context as a major link between different sites or different parts of a very large **network** system on the same site.

Internet browser This is the **software** used to read **HTML** and other pages on the **Internet**. When people surf the net they could be using an Internet browser like Microsoft's Internet Explorer or Netscape's Navigator, for example.

Internet domain name An Internet domain name is *a category for registration of* **Internet web sites** *belonging to particular organisations or individuals.* An Internet domain name like 'www.mywebsite.com' is much easier to remember than the actual **IP address** used to *connect* the computers on the Internet. A **top-level domain** like '.com' is used to identify the type of organisation or a geographical location. Internet domain names must be registered with an **Internet registrar** *before* they can be set up and propagated to the **root servers** and **name servers** on the **Internet**.

Internet protocol This is a **protocol** *used on the* **Internet** *for low-priority communications in which* **bandwidth** is *not* guaranteed. It is a **packet-switching** protocol and thus no previous setting up is required between the two host computers.

Internet registrar A company, like http://www.networksolutions.com, for example, that *provides a service to other companies and individuals* owning **web sites**. *An Internet registrar holds information regarding who owns what, their names and addresses, and also registers the* **Internet domain names** *so that they may be used on the* **Internet**. Any new site must be added to the **Internet registry** *before* it can be used, otherwise it would not get propagated around the Internet.

Internet registry This registry is *a* **database** *of* **DNS** *information built up by the* **Internet registrars**. VeriSign, for example, is the *only* company allowed to keep *the definitive listing* of all the '.com' companies and individuals, and the **IP addresses** needed for use by the **domain name system**. These registries are updated each day and published to the **root servers**, which in turn get used for transferring information to many other **name servers**.

Internet relay chat This is a *real time chat system* on the **Internet**. A group of people will usually participate in a chat session, usually on some particular topic. The topics change frequently but some, like talking about particular aspects of computers, for example, can go on for a long time. There are thousands of channels and even more topics to choose from.

Internet security software This is the general term for **software** which helps prevent **hacking** or annoying 'features' like **spyware**, **key logging software** and other pests. Typical systems are very similar in operation to virus protection software in that they regularly download **file** updates to help fight off the latest perceived threat. You should compare this with the terms **firewall** and **anti-virus software**.

Internet Service Provider These are the *companies*, like AOL, CompuServe or MSN who allow users to connect to the **backbone** of the **Internet** via *their* computer systems. They would normally provide a range of services like web hosting, **mailboxes**, **news servers** and provide a **name server** which is used to resolve Internet addresses into **IP addresses** used for routing. They also **cache** many popular sites to speed up Internet access for their users.

Internetworking This is the name given to the *connection of two or more* **networks**. Computers communicate with each other via **routers**, **bridges** and **gateways**, usually by making use of the **TCP/IP** set of **protocols**. The **Internet** is the largest example of internetworking, but the term also applies to local area networks (**LAN**) where two or more networks operate together in this way. Most large LANs are examples of internetworking.

Interpreter This is **software** that converts a **high-level language** into **machine code** and executes it *just one line at a time*. It is *used within an interactive environment*, where the user gets instant feedback when running the program. **BASIC** is the best example of an interpreted language, although some versions may be compiled using a **compiler**. Interpreters are slow compared with compilers, but are less frustrating to use when programs are being developed, because errors may be corrected more easily.

Interrupt The name given to the process whereby the *operations currently being carried out* by a **microprocessor** are *interrupted*, so that something more important may be done. *When the interrupt has been serviced, the interrupted task may then be reinstated.* Interrupts are common in **software** like **operating systems**, and are controlled with the aid of a **data structure** called a **stack**.

Interrupt This is a signal from a device (or **software**) seeking the attention of the **microprocessor**. The **interrupt register** is checked at the end of the **fetch-execute cycle**. Assuming the **interrupt priority** is sufficiently high; the processor will finish the **current instruction**, dump the appropriate **registers** (**PC**, **accumulator** etc.) onto the **stack**, and then jump to the **interrupt handling routine**. After the interrupt handling routine has done its job, the microprocessor retrieves the register contents back from the stack, and continues with what it was doing before the interrupt occurred. This is achieved by the use of a 'RETURN' instruction at the end of the code which handles the interrupt.

Interrupt flag A special **bit** inside the **flag register**, which might be set to '1' if an **interrupt** *has* occurred or set to '0' if an interrupt has *not* occurred.

Interrupt handler See **interrupt handling routine**.

Interrupt handling routine The interrupt handling routine or interrupt handler is *a* **program** *designed to service an interrupt*. When an **interrupt** occurs (e.g. the real-time clock might need updating) the interrupt handler will handle this task, then pass control back to what the **microprocessor** was previously doing.

Interrupt priorities **Interrupts** *are usually assigned priorities depending on their importance*. Higher-priority interrupts are usually serviced first, with the lower-priority interrupts taking their turn. If an interrupt is already being serviced and a higher-priority one occurs, then the interrupt currently being executed will itself be interrupted, and the higher priority one gets serviced first. Many interrupts with different levels of priority can occur simultaneously, and the system is managed by using a *special queue* called a **LIFO stack**.

Interrupt register A **register** which holds details about the **interrupts** being handled by the system.

Interview One of the methods **systems analysts** *use for fact finding when developing systems*. Interviews need to be well structured and documented if useful outcomes are to be gained from the information. Standard interviews are often used when carrying out **feasibility studies** regarding potential computer-based solutions to a problem. You should make use of documented interviews in your A2 computer science projects.

Intranet This is a collection of computers, under the control of an institution, set up to give similar functionality to that provided by the **Internet**. *Only people belonging to a particular company or educational institution may use the intranet because it is private*, and not necessarily available to the public. Individual members of the institution *may* access the *private intranet* from *outside of the company* by using a **VPN**.

IP See **Internet protocol**.

IP address An *address used to uniquely locate a particular computer or other device* on a **network**. An IP address consists of four numbers like 10.62.127.36. However, not all combinations are permitted, and most have already been assigned! These numbers are used by **routers** to steer data over the **Internet** or a **LAN**. Each computer connected to the Internet must have a unique number, but computers on a LAN behind a **proxy server** look just like one computer to the Internet (having the IP address of the proxy server). As we are running out of numbers in the current format, numbers are usually dynamically allocated to users making use of a **dial up connection**, and then dropped when the user releases the line. A new system of addressing is currently being developed, but implementing it may be a long, complex and expensive process.

IRC See **Internet relay chat**.

ISO See **International Standards Organisation**.

ISO OSI model The **International Standards Organisation** Open Systems Interconnection model is *a 7-layer system for the interconnection of computer networks*. The layered model enables different systems to be integrated with others more easily without having to change every component in the whole system. It consists of a range of **protocols**, which collectively form what is called a **protocol stack**. Without models such as this, computers would not be able to communicate with each other unless individual manufacturers agreed on the methods to be used.

ISP See **Internet Service Provider**.

Iteration Iteration means *looping*, i.e. doing *the same thing over and over again*. 'FOR-TO-NEXT' and 'REPEAT UNTIL' **control structures** would be examples of iteration, where the same operations are repeatedly carried out on **program statements** contained within these **loop** structures.

Java An **object-oriented programming** language that is compiled into an intermediate code called **intermediate byte code**. It is this intermediate byte code which compiles on the client's machine. It is designed to be **platform** independent, which means that Java code should run on a variety of different computers with different **operating systems**.

Java applet A Java applet is a *very small* **Java** *application that runs in a suitably enabled* **web browser**. Java applets typically give users' web browsers lots of additional functionality, and enable really fancy interaction and animations to take place. Running some Java applets can be quite dangerous, because they can read and write information to the files on your computer. Options are available to separate Java applets into ones from sources that can be trusted, and others that are not trusted. Memory space available to Java applets is usually limited to a defined area in which they can run, thus offering some protection on the client machine.

Java servlet This is a **Java applet** *which is designed to run on a* **web server**.

Java virtual machine This is **software** *running on a computer which translates* **Java** *programs written in* **intermediate byte code**, *into the code that can be run on a particular machine.* Many different **platforms** are able to run Java programs because the Java virtual machine carries out this translation process. Java is therefore a platform independent language. Modern **web browsers** usually provide a Java virtual machine environment which can run Java applets to increase interactivity and functionality on a web page.

JavaScript JavaScript is a **scripting language** that adds interactive functionality to **html web pages**. Do not confuse JavaScript with **Java**, which is a fully **object-oriented programming language**.

JCL See **job control language**.

Job control language This *is the language used to control a* **batch** *of jobs in a* **batch-operating system** *environment.* Typically this language would be used to control what jobs are run and when, what resources may be used, and aid any charging mechanism that might need to be imposed for accounting purposes. A job control language is typically used in a **mainframe computer** environment.

Joystick This is a hand-held input **peripheral** in which a *stick is used to control movement* and other parameters. It is one of the basic input tools for controlling games like 'flight simulators', or other games of the 'shoot-em-up' variety. You should realise that there are also *many serious uses* for joysticks, like surgeons carrying out remote surgery via robotic arms placed at remote locations. The surgeon may control a robot by using a joystick interface.

Kbyte See **Kilobyte**.

Key escrow This is a **strong encryption** system whereby *a copy of your* **private key** *is given to the government!* This system is supposed to enable governments to help track criminals and to give legal users 'peace of mind'. However, the widespread use of strong encryption like **PGP** has ensured that this is unlikely to be successful.

Key field This is also called a **primary key field**. In a **file** or a **database** table, this is *the* **field** which *uniquely identifies* a particular **record**. E.g. in a library database, the book table or file might have a key field of 'ISBN number', or for a customer database, the key field might be 'customer account number'. See also **composite key field**.

Key logging software This is **software**, sometimes put onto a computer by a **hacker**, *which monitors key strokes on the keyboard and then e-mails this information back to the hacker*. This is one of the most serious threats to a computer system, because **passwords** and other confidential information may be obtained. **Internet security software** may be installed to help prevent this happening.

Key words In a **programming language**, a key word is a *reserved word which has special meaning* to the language translator. These key words are translated into **machine code** by the **interpreter** or **compiler**. As an example, if **BASIC** is being used; for the program statement 'WHILE perimeter < 10 DO', the key words are 'WHILE' and 'DO', and the word 'perimeter' is interpreted as a **variable**. Key words *can't be used in any other context*, or the meaning of the language statement may be misinterpreted.

Keyboard The main **input device** used for manually entering **data** into a computer. A variety of keyboards exist to reduce **RSI**, and modern keyboards have a plethora of extra functionality like 'special keys for the **web**' or to 'control multimedia devices'.

Kilobyte One Kilobyte = 1,024 **bytes** of data. In other branches of science 1K means 1000, but *in computing, when storage devices are being considered, 1024 is more convenient* because it is a **binary** multiple. The system is carried on in this way when using **Megabyte**, **Gigabyte** and **Terabyte** etc. You should note that *this system applies only to bytes* of data.

Knowledge This term is used to distinguish the increased sophistication of a **knowledge base** system compared to simply storing **data** or **information**. *New knowledge can often be inferred from the knowledge already programmed into the system*. A knowledge base holds all the **facts** and **rules** which are programmed into the system using a language like **Prolog**.

Knowledge base This is the **software** used to generate **knowledge** from known **facts** and **rules** using a **logic programming** language like **Prolog**.

Knowledge base This is *a 'database' of* **rules** *and* **facts** *set up in a* **logic programming** *language*. An alternative name for a knowledge base is an **expert system**. The knowledge base is built up by providing a set of **clauses** (rules) from which a language like **Prolog** can infer if facts contained within the knowledge base are 'true' or 'false'. When using this method we can concentrate on the **declarative** view of the problem and not on how the solution might be obtained. Typical uses of knowledge-based systems are 'medical systems', 'oil exploration' and 'psychological analysis'.

Label An optional part of an **assembly language** instruction which is used as a reference, often for the purposes of jumping to a particular part of a **program**. Some **high-level languages** also support the use of labels.

LAN See **Local Area Network**.

Laptop A portable computer which is powered by internal batteries. Modern powerful laptops have much of the functionality and power of a good desktop **PC**. This term should be compared with a **palmtop** and a **PDA**.

Laser printer This is a **page printer** which works on the *same principle as a photocopier*. It is very high quality, and the larger laser printers are capable of producing reasonably high volumes like 30 to 60 pages a minute or more. Laser printers are available both in colour and black and white. They are *more expensive to buy* compared with **ink jet printers**, but they are *less expensive to run* in terms of the cost/page. This is because ink jet printer cartridges are expensive.

Layer 1 See the **physical layer** of the **ISO OSI model**.

Layer 2 See the **data link layer** of the **ISO OSI model**.

Layer 3 See the **network layer** of the **ISO OSI model**.

Layer 4 See the **transport layer** of the **ISO OSI model**.

Layer 5 See the **session layer** of the **ISO OSI model**.

Layer 6 See the **presentation layer** of the **ISO OSI model**.

Layer 7 See the **application layer** of the **ISO OSI model**.

LCD displays This is a Liquid Crystal Display. It is typical of displays used on flat-screen colour **monitors** for portable computers. It is much less heavy than a conventional computer display (**VDU**), and uses considerably less power. This technology has now become available for larger displays making them suitable for use with an audience of a few tens of people.

LCD panel display A device, based on **LCD display** technology, which enables a conventional OHP (Over Head Projector) to be used to show computer output on a large screen. The LCD panel is *placed on top of the OHP base* where the teacher or lecturer would normally do the writing. The quality of these devices does not match the quality of good **projection systems**.

Leaf node The last **node** in a **tree structure** and therefore it has *no children*. A leaf node is the same as a **terminal node**.

Leased line networking This is a *private communication channel* that is *permanently connected* between two systems. It is used by companies in preference to making use of **dial up networking** (**dial up connection**) where phone bills may be incurred for every call. It is usual to pay a *monthly* or an *annual fee* to the telecoms company who provides this link. The **bandwidth** (**baud rate**) available on a leased line can be anything from about 128 Kbit/sec to a few Mbit/sec or more.

Least significant bit *The bit within a number having the least value*. As an example, for the pure binary number 10110011 the rightmost '1' is the least significant because it has a value of 1.

Left pointer This concept is used in a **binary tree data structure**. It is *a number* (**vector**), *often stored along with the* **node** *data, which points to the left-hand* **child node**. On a tree diagram a **pointer** is represented by an arrow.

LEP displays This is a display making use of Light Emitting Plastic or Light Emitting Polymers. These displays are literally *flexible*, and can thus be rolled up or shaped to any background. Technologies making use of these displays in the future could range from huge wall-mounted displays down to roll up computers that fit in your pocket just like a piece of paper.

Library These are *prewritten routines which may be called up at run time*. An **assembler** would usually link any library routines and **macros** during the assembly process, and a **compiler** would usually link to these libraries during the compilation process. Many libraries are written by **third parties**.

Library programs This is a suite of routines which are available to be called from other **programs**. These programs or routines usually carry out common tasks such as 'graphics', 'communications' or 'input/output', for example. Without these it would take much longer to develop complex **software**, because **programmers** would need to reinvent the wheel each time they write a new program. **Third parties** also provide an extensive range of library programs for different **high-level languages**, **low-level languages** and some **applications**.

LIFO A Last-In-First-Out **data structure** in which the last data item entered is the first data item to be processed. It is the same data structure as a **stack**.

LIFO stack An *area of* **memory** *set up to act as a LIFO (Last In First Out)* **data structure**. Unlike a **queue**, the last item of data placed onto the stack is the first item to be taken off the stack. A LIFO stack is useful for handling **interrupts** because the interrupt may be processed, and control passed back to the previous task very easily by using this method. This is done by saving the contents of important **registers** onto the **stack** before the interrupt, and restoring the registers by removing them from the stack after the interrupt has been serviced. A LIFO stack is also extremely useful when carrying out **recursion** for the same reasons.

Light pen This is a pen which can be used for *choosing items on the screen or for drawing, by moving the pen over the screen*. It is sometimes useful for certain **applications** like **art packages** and **CAD packages**, but has now been largely superseded by the pens used in combination with a **graphics tablet**.

Line printers These are *impact printers* that print a single line at a time. They are often used in the **minicomputer** and **mainframe computer** environment, because they can support **fan-fold stationery** and are also very fast, thus coping easily with large volumes of data.

Linear list This is *a* **data structure** *which represents an ordered set of elements*. A linear list does *not* have to be in any *particular* order. Typically a linear list might be the result of **transactions** carried out in a business in the order in which these transactions occurred. These transactions would be stored in a **transaction file**.

Linear queue A **data structure** *based on the* **FIFO** *principle, in which the beginning and end of the* **queue** *are implemented by* **pointers**. A conventional queue would have both start and end pointers, but a problem occurs when large numbers of items have been processed, because the queue structure has a natural tendency to creep down in memory. A **circular queue** gets over this limitation.

Linear search This is a very simple **search algorithm**. *A list is examined one element at a time, until the desired item is found, or found not to be in the original list.*

Linked list This is a list of data which is managed by a system of **pointers**. A pointer is stored along with the node data that points to the next item in the list. A free space list is set up enabling extra items to be added to the original list. This is done by manipulation of the pointers in the linked list and free space list.

List (1) This is the general name for a one-dimensional **array** which contains data elements in the form of a list. See **linear list**.

List (2) A **list** in the language **Prolog** is represented as having a **head** and a **tail**. A list can be empty, but is usually made up from many elements.

Local Area Network A Local Area Network is *a collection of* **computers** *connected to a* **network**, *usually to share information and other resources*. A **LAN** is often under the control of an individual organisation like a business or educational institution. A LAN does not make use of the public telecommunication systems. LANs vary in size from two or three computers found in the home, to thousands of computers that may be spread over a campus for many kilometres. Large LANs will have multiple resources including **file servers**, **proxy servers**, **intranet servers** and **printer servers**, for example.

Local machine The **machine** you are currently using. It is a term commonly applied to a **fat client** on a **network**.

Local variable In programming, a **variable** that *does not exist outside of a particular* **subroutine** *or* **procedure**. Its value can't be altered by any code outside of these procedures, and the same variable name may be independently used in other subroutines or procedures without any interaction. Compare with the term **global variable**.

Log on name See **user name**.

Logic programming This **programming paradigm** *concentrates on the descriptive side of relationships*. To produce an output we ask a set of questions by defining **queries** to interrogate a **knowledge base**. Logic programming does not require the user to provide **imperatives** regarding how the problem should be solved. *This level of abstraction enables the* **programmer** *to concentrate on the solution, rather than the methods needed to produce a solution*. A good example of logic programming is **Prolog**, where sets of **facts** and **rules** are used to define the **knowledge base**.

Logical drive A **logical drive** is a disk image in which the user of the computer *thinks that they have two or more physical disk drives*. It is common to split up a very large drive into a number of logical partitions, and assign a letter to each. After **partitioning**, a user might have a 'C:', 'D:' and 'E:' drive, which can then be used as if they were *three separate physical drives* as far as the **operating system** is concerned. A **mapped network drive** would also present the user with the illusion that they have another hard disk drive, and this is another example of a *logical drive*. In practice, a mapped network drive is probably just a **directory** on a **file server** connected to the **LAN**.

Logical error An *error in the logic of the* **program**. A program may be syntactically correct (i.e. no **syntax errors**) but may still not work as expected. A **dry run** or similar **debugging** technique may be used to determine exactly where the error lies. The error could easily be a mistake in the original **algorithm** from which the code has been developed, and this should therefore be checked too. This term should be compared with a **syntax error**.

Logical expression *A logical expression can only take on a value which is true or false*. A **program statement** like 'IF x = 1 AND y = 1 THEN z = 2' contains the logical expressions 'x = 1' and 'y = 1' which, because of the AND function, if both are evaluated to be true, then Z is put equal to the value of 2, otherwise the result will be false, in which case the value of Z is not altered.

Logical operation *Operations such as* **AND**, **OR**, **NOT** *and* **XOR** etc. These operations are carried out on individual **bits** held inside **registers**. Each bit inside one register is usually grouped with the equivalent bit in another register and the result of the logical operation is put into the **accumulator**. These logical operations are *also available* in most

high-level languages, and can be used to operate on **binary** or **hexadecimal codes**.

Logical schema See **conceptual schema**.

Logical shift This is a term normally associated with **assembly language**. A **shift** *operation in which the sign of the number contained inside the register is not preserved*. This term should be compared with an **arithmetical shift** operation.

Loop In programming, a loop structure is *a structure like* 'FOR-TO-NEXT', 'DO WHILE' or 'REPEAT UNTIL'. The use of 'loop structures' makes for concise and efficient **program code**, because *the program statements contained within these loops may be repeated many times over*.

Low-level language These are the **assembly languages** and **machine code** which are far removed from the way that humans normally think, but very close to the way in which a particular type of computer operates. Assembly language or machine code programs for one type of computer (like a **Mac**) will *not* operate on another type of computer (like a **PC**), because the **microprocessors** inside each machine are not compatible due to the different **instruction sets**.

MAC address This is the Media Access Control address. It is basically the hardware address of a computer (or other device) attached to a **network**. It consists of six hex numbers separated by colons like '90:00:75:02:01:FC', for example. **Switches** or **intelligent hubs** may use the MAC address of a computer to decide whether or not it can connect to the network for security reasons.

Machine Another name for a **computer**.

Machine code The **binary** code used by a particular **microprocessor** to carry out fundamental operations like 'ADD', 'LOAD' or 'STORE'. Different families of microprocessor have different machine code or **instruction sets**. This means that machine code designed for one type of **machine** will *not* work on any other type.

Machine oriented language This is a **programming language** which is close to the fundamental ways in which a particular **machine** (computer) operates. Typical of this would be the set of **machine code** instructions for a particular **microprocessor**. Compare this term with **human oriented language**.

Machine readable **Data** that can only be read by a machine. An example of this is a **binary file**. This should be compared with the term **human readable**.

MacOS Apple's **operating system** for the Mac computers. These computers provide an alternative to the dominant **PC**.

Macro (1) This is a term normally associated with **assembly language**. A macro *is a sequence of instructions which can be called up by using just one instruction*. Each of these 'macro instructions' would then be converted into the **machine code** which they represent. This saves the **programmer** the task of having to write the same code several times.

Macro (2) *A macro can be created by recording a sequence of actions in an* **application package** *like a* **word processor** *or a* **spreadsheet**, for example. These actions, undertaken by the user, are converted into a **macro language**, which can then be run by clicking over the macro name (i.e. by running the same sequence of actions to those originally recorded). *If a* **programmer** *is familiar with the macro language for a particular application, then whole routines may be written without recourse to going through the recording process.* See **Visual Basic for Applications**.

Macro language A **fourth-generation language** *which is used to control actions* in **applications** like **word processors**, **databases** and **spreadsheets**. On the Microsoft Office Suite, the macro language is **VBA**, or **Visual Basic for Applications**.

Magnetic Ink Character Recognition The system used at the bottom of bank cheques where *special ink, forming the human readable characters at the bottom of a cheque, is magnetised* so that these numbers can be read by an **MICR reader**. Without this technology millions of bank cheques could not be cleared so quickly each day.

Magnetic tape See **tape**.

Mail merge A technique used by **software** such as **word processors** to produce a number of similar documents (like a standard letter) when used in conjunction with a **database** (sometimes contained within the word processor system) usually containing information like 'names and addresses'. This is one of the techniques to generate 'personalised junk mail' sent out to millions of homes.

Mail reader *A* **program** *which reads* **electronic mail**. It also enables the user to construct and send e-mail, to add **attachments**, manage address books and carry out other useful tasks. Typical examples of mail readers are Microsoft's Outlook Express and Netscape's Messenger.

Mail server A network **file server** (computer) whose function is to receive, store and send **e-mail** messages. A mail server can be thought of as the equivalent to the post office, where e-mails are stored until the user is ready to log on and receive them.

Mailbox A place on a **disk** on a **mail server** which holds **electronic mail** for a particular user. The **e-mail address** of the user determines which mailbox is to be used.

Main memory A term used for primary storage like **RAM** and **ROM**.

Mainframe computer A large computer, typical of those housed in environments like the head office of a bank or a utility company, where millions of **transactions** take place during a single day. Mainframes can also be found within some university computer departments. Most mainframes can deal with hundreds of users simultaneously connected to the system, usually by using a **time sharing system**. **Users** may be connected to a **mainframe** computer via a **terminal** or a **PC** running terminal-emulation software. These computers typically have extremely large storage capacities and many **peripheral** devices, but smaller mainframes could have a modest number of users and peripherals.

Maintenance Once a system has been fully commissioned it's likely that *the odd* **bug** *will come to light that needs to be fixed. Also, the changing needs of the user* might require the system to be altered in some way which was not envisaged at design time. *Tinkering with a completed system like this is known as maintenance.* If too much maintenance is being undertaken, then a new and more appropriate system should be considered.

Maintenance of tree structures This refers to the act of *adding* or *deleting* **nodes** from a **tree structure**. Standard **algorithms** are available which maintain **ordered tree structures** like **binary trees**.

Managed hub A **hub** *which has some intelligence built into it.* It is possible to **route** data more effectively or to perform diagnostics over the **network** from a remote computer. In large installations managed hubs form an essential part of keeping the network running effectively. Some managed hubs have now become so sophisticated, that they can perform a variety of **routing**, **bridging** and **switching** functions all from within the same unit. They are central to the management of very large and complex networks.

Mantissa This represents the *fractional part* of a **floating point number**. This number is then modified by using the value in the **exponent** to give the *actual value* of the **floating point number**.

Many-to-many relationship In **relational database** design, this is *a mapping such that many instances (examples) of a particular* **entity** *are mapped onto (or associated with) many instances of another entity*. A typical example of a many-to-many relationship would be 'many students' may study 'many courses'. Many-to-many relationships *can't* be set up in a relational database, and therefore they are modelled using many **one-to-many relationships**.

Mapped network drive See **logical drive**.

MAR See **Memory address register**.

Mark scheme A list provided by the AQA board which outlines what they are looking for in an **A2 project**. The A2 mark scheme consists of **analysis**, **design**, **technical solution**, **system testing**, **system maintenance**, **user manual**, **appraisal** and **quality of communication**.

Mark sense reader This is the system where *marks made with an HB pencil or a black Biro* can be read into a mark sense reader machine. A common use for this system is dealing with the responses to multiple-choice examination questions. Candidates fill in special boxes to represent their candidate number, and then fill in special boxes indicating the answers they wish to give from a selection of possible answers for each question. This system enables examination boards to automatically mark thousands of papers very quickly in a **batch**, with little need for human intervention. See **OMR**.

Mark-up language A language like **HTML** (**HyperText Mark-up Language**) or XML (Extensible Mark-up Language), which belong to *a class of more generalised mark-up languages, the purpose of which is to define the relationship between the content of a document and the way it is laid out.* Most students should have experience of **HTML**, and the use of <tags> to switch **attributes** (like bold or italic) on, and other </tags> to switch them off.

Mask A *pattern of* **bits**, *usually used with the aim of blocking out or enabling other bits inside a* **register** or **Boolean variable** in a **program**. As an example, if the 'mask 11110000' is used together with an **AND** function on the number '10111100', then the *four most significant bits* of the number are *not altered* but the *four least significant bits are set to zero*. Hence the number 10111100 becomes 10110000 after masking it with the bit pattern (mask) 11110000.

Masking A technique where a **mask** (pattern of **bits**) is used in conjunction with **logical operations** like '**AND**' and '**OR**' to alter the original pattern of bits to perform some function like switching bits on and off without altering the other bits. This is useful to **set** or **reset** some bits inside a **register** without altering other bits.

Master file A **data file** which contains the *most up-to-date information* available. It is usual to update the master file by using a **transaction file**, and the result of this operation is a new master file. Several generations of master file are often kept just in case any errors occur when updating takes place, when these files may be used to help recover a previously held set of data.

Mbyte See **Megabyte**.

MDR See **Memory data register**.

Media Access Control See **MAC address**.

Megabyte One Megabyte = 1024 × 1024 = 1,048,576 **bytes** of data. It should be abbreviated as MB and not Mb. (Mb represent M**bits**, although you will see references to this which are obviously meant to be Megabytes!) See **Kbyte**.

Members This is a term used in **object-oriented programming**. Members are the **attributes**, of a particular class. E.g. a terminator-robot class may have attributes like 'rotary cannons' and 'laser guided missiles'. See also **method**.

Memory This is **hardware** that can *store data*. It is most commonly used to refer to **primary storage** devices like **RAM** and **ROM**, when it should be referred to as main memory. It can also be applied to **secondary storage** devices like **floppy disks**, **hard disks** and **tape** etc.

Memory address register This **register** holds the **address** of the **data** (or **assembly language** instruction) that is currently being accessed. *It holds the address of the location in* **memory** *from where data is to be fetched or the location in memory to where data should be sent.*

Memory data register This is a **register** *that holds the* **data** *that was either read from or written to the memory the last time that a read/write operation took place.* The memory data register will therefore hold both **assembly language** instructions and data. If the data is an assembly language instruction, it will be transferred to the **Current Instruction Register** at a later stage in the **fetch-decode-execute** cycle.

Memory management This is dealing with processes like the allocation and distribution of **memory** appropriate to the **tasks** being run, managing **virtual RAM** by swapping pages of memory to **disk**, or creating appropriate size **buffers**, for example. Tasks like this are controlled by the **operating system** and by the computer **hardware**.

Memory map A picture (*map*) *showing how parts of the computer's* **memory (RAM)** *are allocated to different* **tasks**. Part of the memory will be used by the **operating system**, parts may be used by **applications** and parts can be reserved for **users' programs**, for example. Other parts of the memory map are allocated to **hardware** like **graphics cards** and **sound cards**.

Menu A menu is a list of available choices of things to do. For example, in **Windows**, the Start Menu gives access to the range of **programs** that can be run. In a **word processor**, a particular drop-down menu might give access to all the formatting commands. Presenting the user with a choice in this way is fundamental to the operation of a **GUI operating system**.

Merging This means joining two ordered sets of **data** (alphabetical order or account number order etc.) to produce a single set of data containing the original two. It is commonly used when carrying out **transaction** processing to produce a new **master file** from the old master file (the first data source) and the **transaction file** (second data source).

Message This is one way of arranging communication *between two computers*. A message is often made up from many **packets**, which are joined together at the receiving end to form the original message. See **packet switching** and **message switching**.

Message switching Message switching, unlike **circuit switching**, does *not necessarily use the same link to transmit different messages*. Message switching is more efficient than circuit switching when sending computer **data**, because the line may be used for other messages if one system is not actually transmitting at any particular moment in time. Because no 'permanent' physical connection is used, and *different routes* may be used for *different messages* between the *same two computers*, this technique is known as establishing a **virtual circuit** or virtual connection.

Meta-search engine This is a search engine which searches **databases** created by *other* search engines, compared with a conventional **search engine** which would create and search its own database. Some search engines, like Copernic, for example, has its own database but can also be enabled as a meta-search engine.

Method This is a term used in **object-oriented programming**. A method is the actions, like **functions** and **procedures**, which are associated with a particular **class**. See also **members**.

MICR See **Magnetic Ink Character Recognition**.

MICR reader A machine which reads the magnetic ink characters after they have been magnetised. It is used by the clearing banks to process the enormous number of cheques that are generated each day.

Micro browser This is the name used for an **Internet browser** intended to be used on a **PDA** or a mobile phone. It does not have all the facilities of a desktop computer browser like Internet Explorer, for example, but enables PDAs and mobile phones to surf some sites on the web very effectively. Other **web sites** are designed with these smaller devices in mind, and make use of **WAP**.

Microcomputer *A computer, usually built around a single* **microprocessor**, *and normally used by one person at any moment in time*. Typical of microcomputers are the **PCs** and **Macs** used in the office, home and educational environments. Some microcomputers do have more than one processor, but these are predominantly found in **file servers** on a **network**, or used for more powerful **workstations** running high-end **CAD packages**.

Microfiche This is *a rectangular photographic card or sheet on which frames of information, usually corresponding to a page of a document, can be displayed*. A **microfiche reader** is needed to display this information.

Microfiche reader A *machine to read photographic documents created on* **microfiche**. This system is typical of that used in libraries for displaying book **data** and in garages for displaying technical data on cars. The advantage of this system is that you do not need a computer to display the data. However, *as computers reduce in price, and with the popularity of* **PDF** *document distribution continuing, this system will probably be made redundant or kept for specialist use only*.

Microfilm This is *a photographic technique for reducing documents in size, and for displaying on a special machine called a* **microfiche reader**.

Microprocessor A *complete* **CPU** *on a single chip*. It is the main chip around which a **microcomputer** is built. **Supercomputers** are also built up from a huge number of microprocessors, and most computers between these two extremes have a varying number of microprocessors controlling them. Typical microprocessors are Intel's Pentium and AMD's Athlon chips.

Microsecond See **μsec**.

MIDI See **Musical Instrument Digital Interface**.

Millisecond See **msec**.

MIME This is an **acronym** for Multipurpose Internet Mail Extensions. It is a system of **encoding data** such that only the first 7 bits of the **ASCII code** are used. All **binary files** must be converted into this form before being sent as **e-mail attachments** which make use of the **SMTP protocol**.

Minicomputer A *computer with facilities between that of a* **microcomputer** *and a* **mainframe** *computer*. Users may be connected to a minicomputer via a **terminal** or a PC running terminal-emulation **software**. Minicomputers are currently found in companies like banks and supermarkets, where a large number of **transactions** need to be handled quickly. A minicomputer is often used as an interface between **network** users using conventional **PCs** and their connections to a mainframe computer.

Mnemonics This is simply an *aid to the memory*. Typical **assembly language** instructions are built up of mnemonics like 'ADD' and 'LOAD' which are much easier to remember than the equivalent strings of **binary digits** to perform the same operations making use of **machine code**.

MO disks This is the name given to a Magneto Optical disk. It is a *removable and rewritable form of storage* that can store about 2.6 **Gigabytes** of **data**. It is thus ideal for some **backup** or **archive** purposes.

Modelling This is a term used when computers simulate 'real life' scenarios by modelling them in a suitable way. A typical example would be the mathematical models used by the treasury to predict what will happen to the British economy if **data** like 'inflation', 'interest rates' or 'unemployment' etc. are changed. **Spreadsheets** are often used as mathematical models when they are programmed to run **what if scenarios**.

Modem This is a **hardware** device used to convert **digital** computer **data** into **analogue** form so that it can be transmitted over a standard telephone line. The name MODEM comes from the terms **MODulation** and **DEModulation**, which describe exactly what the device does. Modern **ADSL** lines use a very different form of modulation, and special **ADSL modems** are required for this higher **bandwidth** connection.

Moderator The *person who is charged with checking your* **A2 project** *work*. He or she will check that your teacher has marked your work according to the **mark scheme**, and check that some of the verifiable claims that you have made in your project are true. If they disagree with the way in which your teacher has marked the work, they can alter the marks to compensate for 'harshness' or 'leniency'.

Modular design This is *splitting up a system into smaller modules*, to make projects easier to design and manage. **Top-down design** is a good example of one type of modular design process.

Modulation The process of *converting a signal into a different form, more suitable for transmission over a communication* **network**. E.g. converting a human voice (an **analogue signal**) into a **digital signal** for sending over a digital communication network like **ATM** or **Ethernet**.

Module testing This means *testing a separate module from a system to see if it works properly when run in isolation from the rest of the system*. Module testing usually precedes **integration testing**. Suitable **test data** must be used to carry out modular testing. This is also known as **unit testing**.

Modulo arithmetic This is sometimes called *clock arithmetic*, because counting in this system is like counting round the face of a clock. Modulo 12, for example, would use 1, 2, 3, 4, 5, 6, 7, 8, 9, 10, 11, 12, 1, 2, 3, 4 etc. Thus '14 Mod 12' is 2, because counting up to 14 on a 12-hour clock ends up on the number 2. To find the result of modulo arithmetic is simple, we divide by the modulus and take the remainder, thus 14/12 = 1 remainder 2, and thus 2 is the answer, confirming the result just obtained by counting round the 12-hour clock system. One use of modulo arithmetic in computing is to limit the range onto which **data** may be mapped – see **hash addressing**.

Monitor An alternative name for a computer monitor, **VDU** or computer screen.

Morality This is basically 'standards of behaviour' or 'concrete activities' that are regarded as acceptable by civilised people. You should appreciate that 'standards of morality' or 'what is right or wrong' in one country may not apply to another, and this provides for a rich source of discussion. This term should be compared with **ethics**.

Most significant bit *The* **bit** *within a number having the greatest value*. As an example, for the pure **binary** number 10110011 the leftmost '1' is the most significant because it has a value of 128.

Motherboard The main electronic circuit board inside a **PC** which houses the **microprocessor**, **memory** and provides the connections for **graphics cards**, **disk drives**, **CD-ROMs** etc.

Mouse A common **input device** used for pointing with the aim of controlling a variety of on-screen functions within a typical **GUI** environment.

msec One thousandth of a second, i.e. 0.001 sec.

Multi-access A term used to denote a system in which more than one user can access the same data 'simultaneously'. See also **record locking** and **concurrent access**.

Multiplexing This is a method of sending *different* signals over the *same* communications link, either simultaneously or one after the other, depending on the methods being used. See **time division multiplexing** and **frequency division multiplexing**.

Multiprocessing Multiprocessing means having *more than one* **processor**. Using this system *you are therefore able to process more than one* **task** *simultaneously*. **Supercomputers** are good examples of multiprocessing systems, with some having as many as 65,000 different processors, thus enabling the system to carry out 65,000 different tasks at exactly the same moment in time. Typically these large multiprocessor computers would be used to forecast the weather, and the tasks being carried out by each of these processors would usually be smaller and similar parts of the same problem.

Multi-programming A multiprogramming environment is one in which the system is able to operate on *more than one* **program** at the 'same time' or *apparently* at the same time. To actually operate on two programs simultaneously you would need two **processors**, and thus you would thus need a **multiprocessing** system. Multiprogramming normally refers to the ability of a system to interleave the execution of two or more programs under the control of the same processor.

Multitasking The ability to be able to handle more than one **task** at the same time, or apparently at the same time. Most modern **operating systems** are multitasking. *This enables us to make use of one* **application** *while the computer is seemingly doing other things*. For example, you could be downloading a **file** from the **Internet** while watching a **DVD** movie. However, *if a computer has only one processor, then it can only do one thing at a time*. Clever multitasking by the operating system, together with the speed of modern computers, lots of **memory** and large **hard disk** capacities, makes it appear that it's handling these events simultaneously. This term should be compared with **multithreading**.

Multithreading This allows an **operating system** to run different **threads** or *different parts of the same program* at the same time, or apparently at the same time. A **multiprocessing** system would be needed to run the threads at exactly the same time. Assuming the code has been written in an appropriate way, a single program would be executed more quickly in a multithreading environment if more than one processor is present. **Time sharing** would be used for multithreading on a single processor system. This term should be compared with **multitasking**.

Multi-user A term used to denote a system which can be used by more than one person 'simultaneously'.

Musical Instrument Digital Interface This is a standard system using **protocols** recognised by *suitably equipped musical instruments*, like keyboards, guitars and even violins. These codes do not represent actual musical notes, but are codes that control notes on a particular instrument, including the 'sounds they will make', the 'attack', 'sustain' and 'decay rates'. A single person can sound like an entire orchestra with the appropriate **MIDI** equipment and computer system in control.

Mutual independence This is a **relational database** term meaning there are no unique associations between two **attributes** in a **table**.

Name server A **file server** on the **Internet** which holds information about *all the current* **web sites** that are registered by the **Internet registrars**. A name server is usually held by **ISPs** like CompuServe or AOL, for example. These name servers resolve the **web site address** into an **IP address** so that computers may be connected to the appropriate web site. Name servers get their information from the definitive **root servers**.

Nanosecond See **nsec**.

Natural language A language like English or French. This should be compared with a **formal language**. *A natural language is context sensitive*, and thus very difficult for a computer to 'understand' using the present technology. **Fifth-generation programming languages** like **Prolog** are making good progress into computerised natural language analysis.

NC See **network computer**.

Nested interrupts This is the name given to the process of handling a new **interrupt** while another interrupt *is already in the process of being handled*. The new interrupt must have a higher **interrupt priority** than the one currently being processed to enable this nesting to happen. If the new interrupt is not of a higher priority then it is placed in a **queue**.

Nesting This is a concept used in programming in which one **loop** or **selection structure** is placed within another **loop** or selection structure. Typical examples of these are the nested 'IF THEN ELSE' structures or the nested 'FOR TO NEXT' structures. You must be careful to obey all the **syntax rules** and make sure that the loops don't overlap in the wrong way.

Network This is the name given to the system, consisting of both **hardware** and **software** which *enables computers to communicate with each other, principally to share information and other resources*. Computer networks are usually categorised into **LAN**s and **WAN**s. To do this you will need an **operating system** that supports networking, an **NIC**, and a suitable communication channel like **Ethernet** or **ATM**.

Network adapter This is a Network Interface Card. See **network card**.

Network card This is the **hardware** used to interface a computer to a **network**. It is plugged into the **bus system** on the **motherboard**, and a **network cable** (or fibre) plugs into the back of the card. It is also called a Network Interface Card (**NIC**) or **network adaptor**.

Network computer *The network computer or* **NC** *is another name for a* **thin client** *computer*. All **applications**, **operating systems** and **data** are stored on a **file server**, thus the maintenance overheads of a network computer or thin client are therefore kept very low. Thin clients work well with 'bread and butter applications' like **word processors** and **spreadsheets**, but are *not good* with **graphics**, **video**, **sounds** and other programs which make *large demands on the processing capability* of the computer system.

Network ID This is the first **byte** of the **IP address** (for a **class A network**), the first two bytes of the IP address (for a **class B network**) or the first three bytes for a **class C network**. Therefore, for a class A network, and an IP address 141.233.12.55, the network ID would be 141. Network IDs enable administrators of **LANs** to segment networks into more manageable sections.

Network layer This is *layer three* of the **ISO OSI model**. This layer assembles **data** into **packets** for transmission over a variety of **networks** and **switches**, and then routes the data. It is this layer that must resolve all the problems that might be encountered with different technologies associated with different networks. Error checking is carried out at this level too. The **network layer** links the **data link layer** to the **transport layer**. The **Internet Protocol** (**IP**) is a good example of a typical use of the network layer.

Network operating system An **operating system** *which supports connectivity to other computers via a computer* **network**. This connectivity is achieved by interfacing to a **network card**, (**NIC**), by providing the set of **protocols** to enable communication (**TCP/IP**, for example), and support for communication with **file servers**, **proxy servers**, networked printers and other shared resources available over the network. Most modern **operating systems** like **Windows** support this mode of operation.

Network segment A network segment is a term used when *splitting up switched* **Ethernet** *into smaller, more manageable sections, which do not interfere with other segments on different parts of the main network structure*. This process is used to manage the available **bandwidth** more effectively. The **IP addresses** are usually used to control machines within a particular **segment** on the network, by use of a **subnet mask**. If machines on one segment wish to communicate with machines on another segment, then a **router** may be used. The term **subnet** is also used in this context.

Network topology This is *the physical connections that go to make up a* **network**. Examples are **bus topology**, **star topology**, **ring topology** and **tree topology** (using **hubs**). Each topology has advantages and disadvantages over the others, in terms of managing **bandwidth** and **security**.

News server A **file server** on the **Internet** *specifically set up to administer* **Usenet newsgroups**. There are many different news servers available on the Internet, some of which are publicly accessible, and others which require that you belong to a particular **ISP** like CompuServe, for example. The newsgroups carried by these news servers differ, with some ISPs filtering illegal newsgroups. There are tens of thousands of different newsgroups available on most news servers covering every conceivable topic.

Newsgroups This is a large subset of **Usenet**, in which topics on any conceivable subject may be posted and read. Tens of thousands of topics ranging from 'sensible things' via 'ridiculous things' through to 'highly illegal things' are to be found in these groups.

NIC This is a Network Interface Card (See **network card**).

Node *A* **data** *element in a* **tree structure** or **linked list**. A node will usually contain one or more items of data, and usually contain a **pointer** or pointers which help to maintain and move around the **data structure**. See **root node**, **brother node**, **sister node**, **parent node** and **leaf node**.

Non-key element In a **relational database**, an **attribute** *that is not part of the* **primary key** *or the* **composite primary key**.

Normal data This term is used for part of your **A2 project** when dealing with **test data**. This data should be used during the **system testing** phase when data expected to work with the system is used. This term should be compared with **erroneous data** and **extreme data**.

Normalisation (1) *Normalisation is used in the creation of a* **relational database**, *to make sure that possible errors are minimised.* A number of normalisation rules can be applied, but only **first normal form**, **second normal form**, **third normal form** and **BCNF** are necessary at A2 level. Without normalisation, it's possible to get many errors occurring in the database, including 'redundant data', 'accidental corruption of data', 'updates being carried out incorrectly' or 'the results of queries being wrong' to name but a few.

Normalisation (2) When **floating point numbers** are used *it is possible to have multiple representations of the same number. To get over this problem and to make sure that the number is displayed with the greatest precision possible* (given the number of bits), *normalisation is used.* Normalisation ensures that *no leading zeros* exist for *positive numbers* (except the **sign bit**) and *no leading ones* exist for *negative numbers* (except the sign bit). All normalised numbers will have a sign bit followed by a **bit** which is the inverse of the sign bit. E.g. if the sign bit is 1 then the next bit must be 0.

NOT (1) This is a **logical operation** which can be used with a **logical expression**. For example, the **program statement** 'x = NOT(z)' may be used to put the value of x to be true if z is false, or put the value of x to be false if Z is true. *The output of a NOT operation will always be the inverse of the input.* Here x and z are **Boolean** variables, which can only take on true or false values.

Not (2) A **logical operation**, *the output of which is the inverse of the input. If a '1' is fed in then a '0' comes out or if a '0' is fed in then a '1' comes out.* This operation can be used on a **register**, in which case a **bit** within the register will be inverted. This operation is usually available in both **high-level languages** and **low-level languages**.

nsec One thousandth of a millionth of a second, i.e. 0.000000001 sec.

Number base *The name given to the base for counting.* E.g. base ten is the decimal system. Computers make extensive use of number bases like **binary** (base two) and **hexadecimal** (base sixteen).

Numeric variable A **variable** which *represents a number.* A numeric variable could be one of a range of different types like **integer** or **floating point**, for example.

Object An object can represent anything in the real world from a 'sausage' to a 'DVD player'. This concept is used in **object-oriented programming** where objects (which can represent *real* or *abstract* things) *consist of entities like* **variables**, **subroutines** *and* **data types**. An object is a particular **instance** of a class.

Object analysis diagram This type of diagram is useful for undertaking an **object-oriented analysis** *before* any **object-oriented programs** are written. For the purposes of A2 Computing they mainly consist of **class diagrams**, which may be further categorised into **association diagrams, inheritance diagrams** and **aggregation diagrams**. You are also expected to use class diagrams to show **class attributes** and **class operations**. If you are undertaking an A2 project involving an object-oriented language like **C++**, **Java** or **VisualBasic.NET**, then you should have these diagrams in the analysis section of your project.

Object code This is *the* **machine code** *that will run on a particular computer*. It is thus the code generated by a **compiler** or an **assembler**.

Object linking and embedding This is a **database** *concept where* **objects** *such as pictures, text, graphs or other* **data** *may be linked to* **applications** *like* **word processors** *and* **spreadsheets**. As an example, if a word processor contains a graph which is related to monthly sales, and if this document is loaded, then the graph will reflect the state of the data in the database, and not the state of the graph the last time the word processed document was saved.

Object-oriented analysis Object-oriented analysis helps you to design the solution to a problem which is to be solved by using **object-oriented programming** or an **object-oriented database**. It does this by helping to classify and visualise the requirements of the problem in terms of methods like 'identification of **classes**', 'identification of **associations** that exist between classes' and 'analysing **inheritance**', for example. A key component of object-oriented analysis is the **Unified Modelling Language** or **UML**. See also **object analysis diagram**.

Object-oriented database A **database** *which is organised by using concepts identical to those used in* **object-oriented programming**. An object-oriented database would therefore arrange the **data** contained within it in term of **objects**, and make use of mechanisms like **inheritance**. This type of database is able to model data in ways very different from the conventional **relational database** model, and is ideally suited to storing and manipulating database objects like music, pictures and videos.

Object-oriented programming *A* **high-level language** *that supports* **objects**, **classes**, **polymorphism**, **encapsulation** *and* **inheritance**. This programming **paradigm** is of paramount importance because it can be used to model objects in the real world much more easily than using **procedural programming** techniques.

Objectives *A list of things which your* **A2 project** *must do*. This list *should contain a number of quantifiable objectives*, which can be demonstrably measured during the project **testing** and **appraisal** phases. It is perfectly acceptable to include things like 'an easy to use interface', but this is much harder to quantify, and all your objectives should *not* be like this.

Observation One of the *methods* **systems analysts** *use for fact finding when developing systems*. By observing the existing system in practice, it is possible to see if things are being done in the ways suggested, or if methods can be improved in the new system.

OCR system *This is an Optical Character Recognition system*. Characters are scanned in as a **bit-mapped image**, and *then converted into a form where the patterns can be recognised*, with the aim of *turning the bit-mapped image into computer readable text*. After this process, corrections may be made, and the page of text just scanned should be in a form that looks as though it has been typed in by using a **word processor**. OCR systems are now very sophisticated indeed, and can deal with multiple columns, precise positioning and different fonts.

Octal This is counting in base eight. The digits used for this number base are {0, 1, 2, 3, 4, 5, 6, and 7}. It is not as popular as the **binary**, **decimal** and **hexadecimal** systems, but you will come across it in some literature.

ODBC See **open database connectivity**.

Odd parity *A method of ensuring* **data integrity** by counting the number of 1s in the data to be transmitted. If there are 'an even number of ones', then an extra 1 is put in as the **parity bit** to make the total number odd. When the data is received, another count is made on the number of 1s that are present, and, if it is odd, the data is assumed to be correct. See **even parity**.

Off-line This is a term used to describe the situation when a resource is not directly accessible to a network or a computer, for example. Tape **backups** and tape **archives** are examples of things which are usually off-line. The term might also be used for **peripheral** devices like printers and scanners too.

Therefore you could say 'a scanner is off-line' if it is switched off or a connection to it is not available for some other reason. Compare with the term **on-line**.

Off-the-shelf software **Software** that is purchased to save writing your own. School administrative packages, wages packages and accounting packages are typical examples of 'off-the-shelf software'. This software can often be customised to a good degree, but might *not be able to fulfil all the customer's requirements*. If this is likely to be a major problem, customers would have to obtain some **bespoke software**.

OLE See **Object linking and embedding**.

OMR (1) See **Optical Mark Reader**.

OMR (2) See **Optical Mark Recognition**.

One-to-many relationship In **relational database** design, this is *a mapping such that only one instance (example) of a particular* **entity** *is mapped onto (or associated with) many instances of another entity*. A typical example of a one-to-many relationship would be the association between a 'Customer' and 'Orders'. This is because one customer might place many orders with a particular supplier.

On-line This is a term used to describe the situation when you are connected to a network, computer or a particular resource. It is also used in the context of connecting to the **Internet**, or if a **peripheral** like a printer or scanner is available for use. Compare with the term **off-line**.

On-line service provider This is a company which gives you access to the **Internet**. They usually rent out their high-speed connections to the **Internet backbone** which is shared between their customers. This should be compared with an **Internet Service Provider** or **ISP**.

On-line shopping This is *purchasing goods on the* **Internet**, *usually by making use of a secure connection like* **https** *or* **SSL** etc. **Credit card** details can be handled with ease, and e-mails may be sent to the purchaser which acts as confirmation of the order. Many companies provide an on-line tracking service for the order, which provides information like 'order being processed', 'out of stock', or 'order has been dispatched', for example. On-line shopping is accounting for an increasing share of day-to-day business of modern economies.

OOA See **object-oriented analysis**.

OODB See **object-oriented database**.

Op code See **operation code**.

Open database connectivity *By using ODBC, live links to data contained within a* **database** *may be made from other systems that support ODBC. Any edits to the database, either from within the database itself or from one of these supporting* **applications** *are reflected throughout the entire system*. A variety of applications may update **data** held in a database that supports ODBC. ODBC should be compared to exporting data from or into an application. Exporting data, typically by using **CSV**, means that the data is immediately out of date if the original data in the database gets updated.

Open systems interconnection This is *a mechanism set up by the* **ISO** *to determine how different machines may be set up to communicate with each other*. It is based on a *seven layer model* where **protocols** are stacked on top of each other, ranging from the **physical layer** at the bottom to the **application layer** at the top.

Operand *Operands usually describe the* **source** *and* **destination** *of the* **data** *for a particular* **assembly language**, **high-level language** *instruction* or the data itself. Typical examples of operands are 'al' and 'bl' in the assembly language instruction 'or al, bl'. Here the 'al and bl **registers**' are the source of the data, and the al register is the destination for the result.

Operating system This is the **software** that *controls virtually all aspects of the operation of the computer*. It is usually loaded from **disk** shortly after the computer has been switched on. It is the operating system that controls all the **hardware**, enables all other software to be run, controls the **security** in terms of who has access to which **files**, manages the user interface (like the **GUI** or **command line**), manages the order in which **tasks** will be carried out, and manages the **multitasking** aspects too. Without the operating system a computer would be virtually unusable. It is the operating system that determines if **applications** designed for one type of computer will run on another. E.g. the **MacOS** is *not* compatible with Microsoft **Windows**, but some applications, like the Microsoft Office Suite have been written for both.

Operating system software See **operating system**.

Operation This is a term used in **object-oriented analysis**. *In* **object-oriented programming** *an operation refers to the* **methods** (*functions and procedures*) associated with a **class**. On a **class diagram**, a class is shown as a square box with three compartments, and the operations belonging to that class are usually listed in the bottom compartment. Typically the object-oriented language **Java** refers to 'operations', and the object-oriented language **C++** refers to 'methods', but either of these terms can be used on a class diagram. See also **object-oriented analysis** and **object analysis diagrams**.

Operation code This is *the* **mnemonic** *used to represent an* **assembly language** *instruction*. Typical op codes might be 'mov', 'add', 'or' and 'and'. Many op codes (operation codes) need to be accompanied by **operands** to enable the assembly language instruction to work.

Operations manual This is part of the **documentation** that might accompany a large computer system. *The operations manual documents operational procedures such as 'preparation of* **data**' *and other manual techniques*. It could document what departments are responsible for different parts of the system, and who takes control of particular processes. If the procedures in the operations manual are followed, then the system should run smoothly.

Optical Mark Reader This is a device for reading marks made on a page, usually with an HB pencil or black biro. It is typical of the readers used for marking multiple choice examination papers with which most students will be familiar. You should note that some systems use **OMR** to stand for **Optical Mark Recognition**, in which case the reader would be an OMR reader. This is a little unfortunate, but does not matter if you are consistent with your terminology when using these terms.

Optical Mark Recognition This is the system which is able to read marks made on a page, usually with an HB pencil. It is typical of the system used for marking multiple choice examination papers with which most students will be familiar. You should note that some systems use **OMR** to stand for an **Optical Mark Reader**. This is a little unfortunate, but does not matter if you are consistent with your terminology when using these terms.

Optical wand This is *the name given to a* **bar code reader** that is shaped like a *pen* or a *magic wand*! The user manually runs the wand across the bar code, and the system is therefore slightly more difficult to use than a conventional bar code scanner. However, the optical wand is a very cost-effective device for low volume use.

OR (1) This is a **logical operation** which can be used to combine **logical expressions**. For example, the **program statement** 'If x = 3 OR y = 2 THEN Z = 4' could be used to put the value of Z = 4, if x is 3 or y is 2 or both of these conditions are true. *If none of these conditions are true then the value of Z does not get altered.* Here the program statement contains the logical (true/false) expressions 'x = 3' and 'y = 2' combined with the logical operation 'OR'.

OR (2) This is a **logical operation**, usually *performed on two* **binary digits** *held inside* **registers**. *The output of an 'OR' operation is a '1' if either or both inputs are '1'.* Two registers can be used to perform the 'OR' operation, and each bit in one register is usually ORed with the equivalent **bit** in the other register, with the answer (the bit pattern obeying the rules outlined here) stored in the **accumulator**. This operation is usually available in both **high-level languages** and **low-level languages**.

ORDER BY This is part of *the terminology used in a* **relational database** *system when a* **query** *is being defined.* 'ORDER BY' is an **SQL key word** used to display the result of a query in some specific order.

Ordered file A **data file**, stored such that the **records** are in some *predetermined order*, like alphabetical or customer ID, for example. The system is ideal for **batch processing**, like the systems used in banking and the utility industry.

Ordered list A list of **data** items which are in some particular order, like numeric or alphabetical. Some search **algorithms**, like the **binary search**, for example, require data to be stored in an ordered list.

OSI OSI or Open Systems Interconnection is *a mechanism for connecting the same or disparate systems to each other via communication networks like* **LANs** *and* **WANs**. A typical example is the **ISO OSI model**.

Output device *Any device designed to get* **data** *out from a computer system.* Thus a **VDU**, **monitor**, **printer** and **plotter** are all examples of output devices.

Overflow If overflow occurs, this means that *a number is too big to fit into the available space for it to be stored.* E.g. the **binary** number for 20 (**base ten**) could not be stored using just 4-**bits**, because 15 is the maximum number that can be stored if only 4 **binary digits** are available and positive **integers** are being used.

Packet This is *a small, self contained unit of information transmitted over* a **network**. It is usually made up of a **header**, the **source address** and **destination addresses**, a **CRC** and other information depending on packet type. Of course we also need the **data** itself. A number of packets will usually make up a **message**, and packets could be transmitted by using many different **routes**; because of this packets don't always arrive at the destination in the correct order, and the receiving computer has to sort this out so that the message makes sense.

Packet switching This is *the same as* **message switching**, *but smaller, well-defined* **packets** *of information are used*. Packet switching utilises the available **bandwidth** more effectively between a large number of computers. Each computer on the network (**LAN** or **WAN**) will therefore get a turn at transmitting information more often compared to message switching.

Page description language This is a **high-level language** for *controlling every attribute of text and graphics that can be printed*. One of the main reasons for using a system like this is that the printer (which must support the language) does all the work, and the system therefore does not rely on the type of computer or the type of fonts installed. Therefore, each person who prints a **Postscript**, (one of the page description languages) document *will see exactly the same thing on their printer regardless of computer type*, **operating system** or installed **software**.

Page printer A **printer** that prints *one page at a time*. This should be compared to a **line printer** (*one line at a time*) or to a **character printer** (*one character at a time* – like a **dot-matrix printer**). Page printers (*laser printers*) form the basis of printers used in the modern office, and high-speed page printers are available for use in the printing industry.

Paging This is *part of a* **memory** *management system that allocates pages (usually numbered) to different programs and* **tasks** *being run by the* **operating system**. It is also the term applied to *swapping* pages of programs and data to and from a **disk** when a **virtual memory** system is being implemented.

Paint package A program specifically *designed to create artistic drawings*. Paint packages usually construct **pixel-based graphics**, but some deal with **vector-based graphics** too, which are more commonly used for **CAD packages**. Typical examples of paint packages are Adobe's PhotoShop and Corel's CorelDraw. See also **art package**.

Palmtop This is a portable computer whose functionality is somewhere between that of a **laptop** and a **PDA**. Palmtop computers may not be able to fit into your pocket like a PDA, and usually have simpler versions of the **application software** available on laptops. This term should be compared with a **laptop** and **PDA**.

Paperwork review *One of the methods* **systems analysts** *use for fact finding when developing systems*. Existing manuals and tracing paper work can often point out ways in which a new system may be improved.

Paradigm The *main method* by which a programming language is organised and categorised. See **programming paradigm**.

Parallel data communication This is **data** communication in which *two or more* **bits** (**binary digits**) of data *are transmitted simultaneously*. This method is used extensively for short-distance communications between the **microprocessor** and **motherboard** (via the **address bus** and **data bus**) and for communications with a **printer** (via the **parallel port**). Synchronisation between the various transmission and reception systems is carried out by means of the **clock** on the **motherboard**. Parallel data communication should be contrasted with **serial data communication**.

Parallel implementation This is *a common technique for implementing a system in which the old and new systems are run in parallel*. It is a very safe option, but it may require more manpower to operate both systems at the same time. Any discrepancies between the old and new systems can be rectified before becoming totally reliant on the new system. If the new system fails, you still have the old system in operation and the business can keep going until the new system is working properly.

Parallel port A **port** on the computer in which communication is achieved by simultaneously sending **binary** data down different wires. A common parallel port on a **PC** is the **printer** port, although the **USB** (a **serial port**) is taking over this role on modern computer systems.

Parameter A parameter is a *value*, usually passed over to a **subprogram** like a **procedure** or **function**. It's important to understand that procedures may have parameters passed over to them using **passing by reference** or **passing by value**. Failure to fully understand this mechanism could have unexpected results when a **program** is executed.

Parent node An *item of* **data** *in a* **tree structure** *that has* **child nodes** (i.e. subordinate nodes branching off from it).

Parity *A method of checking the* **integrity** *(correctness) of* **data**. Parity uses an extra **bit** added on to the original bit pattern. There are two methods, called **odd parity** and **even parity**.

Parity bit A **bit** added on to the **data** to be transmitted and used as a **parity** check for **data integrity** purposes.

Parity checking A *simple method* of ensuring the **integrity** of **data** by means of using **parity**.

Partition *A partition is a part of a* **hard disk** *sectioned off such that it forms a* **logical drive**. Partitioning is useful for organising a very large disk into a number of smaller logical units, which appears to the user to be the same as several smaller physical hard disks. To the **operating system** this partition appears as if you have another **disk** which is called a **logical drive**.

Partitioning (1) The act of splitting up a **hard disk** into a number of smaller partitions which look, both to the **user** and **operating system**, as if there are a number of physical hard drives. Each partition is called a **logical drive**.

Partitioning (2) This is *the name given to the system that divides the computer* **memory** *into manageable sections*. This enables the **operating system** to dynamically allocate set amounts of memory to **programs** and **applications** that are running in a **multitasking operating system**. There are two main methods of achieving this, called **fixed partitioning** and **variable partitioning**.

Pascal A well structured **high-level language**. It is named after the famous mathematician Blaise Pascal, who did much pioneering work in computing. More recent versions of Pascal are called **Delphi**, which provides a visual interface in ways similar to Microsoft's **Visual Basic** and **Visual Basic.NET**.

Passing by reference If a **parameter** is passed to a procedure 'by reference', then *the variable which was passed over to this procedure will have been referenced and have its value altered too*. Programmers should understand the **defaults** used for parameter passing in the **high-level language** they are using. Compare with **passing by value**.

Passing by value When **parameters** are passed over to a **procedure** 'by value', only the value of the variable is passed, and *the original variable is therefore not altered*. Programmers should understand the **defaults** used for parameter passing in the **high-level language** they are using. Compare with **passing by reference**.

Password This is *a secret word or phrase used to gain entry to private* **data**. You should ensure that your passwords are easy to remember but difficult to crack. A password should *not* be a single word in English or indeed any other language, as this could be subject to a **dictionary attack**. Choose something like 'Big_Wobbly_Belly' which would not be found in any dictionary, but is very easy to remember. Many passwords have to obey complexity rules, such as a mixture of upper case, lower case, punctuation and numbers, for example.

Patch A small program, usually intended for the purpose of correcting a **bug** or fixing some security loophole that might not have been appreciated when the original **software** was designed. Users may download the most up-to-date patches from the **Internet**, but larger patches or complete service packs (containing many patches) are also available on CD-ROM from manufacturers like Microsoft.

Path name This is the name given to *locate a resource such as a* **file** *or* **folder** on a **hierarchical directory structure** on a **disk**, **network** or other suitable device.
E.g. K:\Publishing\Nelson Thornes\5th Edition\Glossary\Glossaryfinal.doc is the path name of this particular glossary on the author's hard drive.

PC A *Personal Computer*. More specifically it refers to computers that use Intel's x86 (Pentiums etc.) **microprocessors** (or their clones like AMD etc.) and **bus architectures**. IBM was the *first* to introduce this term, and thus PCs are said to be IBM compatible. However, great strides have been made since the original IBM PC was invented, and powerful 64-**bit** processors and **operating systems** are now available too.

PC See **program counter**.

PDA See **Personal Digital Assistant**.

PDF See **Portable Document Format**.

Peer to peer networking This is a method of organising a **network** *without the need for a* **file server**. Clients on the network share their own resources with others by allowing them to access their hard disks. *Peer to peer networking is not suitable for well organised networks in large organisations* as it opens up security risks and the potential of work not being backed up properly. It is, however, ideal for home networking where members of the family may share a printer and some disks. Compare with the term **client server networking**.

Peripheral Any *device connected to the periphery* of the main computer system. In the **mainframe-computer** days, peripherals were easy to identify, because they *were* on the periphery of the main cabinet housing the **CPU**. In today's PCs, students often think that **disks** and **CD-ROMs** etc. are not peripheral devices because they are housed inside the **base unit**. Today, *any device for input, output or storage* connected to the **motherboard** (apart from the **main memory**, and the **interface cards**, like **graphics cards**, **USB** cards, sound cards and video cards etc.) is a peripheral device.

Perl Although a full computer **programming language** in its own right, *Perl is extensively used as a* **scripting language** *to write* **CGI scripts** *that run on* **Internet servers**.

Personal Computer See **PC**.

Personal Digital Assistant This is a small hand-held device which acts as a personal organiser, simple computer (e.g. it might have **word processing**, **spreadsheet** and **database software**), and has a whole host of other features from mobile telephones to satellite navigation depending on the complexity of the device. It is usual to be able to synchronise these devices with your computer via a cradle, an infra red system or a wireless-based system like Bluetooth.

Personal Information Manager This is **software** that *replaces a conventional desk-top diary*. It provides functions like 'managing appointments', providing a 'calendar', keeping contacts like 'address books' and often manages **e-mail** too. A good example of a **PIM** is Microsoft's Outlook.

PGP See **Pretty good privacy**.

Phased implementation This is *a common technique for implementing a system in which parts of the new system are phased in over time*. Not all systems are amenable to this method, but systems in which old parts may work together with the new are ideal. Typical of this might be a school administration system where 'examination entries', 'reporting' and 'personnel records', for example, might be computerised at different moments in time. This method has the advantage that only a small part of the system is likely to go wrong at any particular moment.

Physical layer This is *layer one* of the **ISO OSI model** *that defines the* **hardware** *and connections*. Typical examples would be the type of **Ethernet** network being used, like 100 Mbit/Sec or Gigabit Ethernet. The physical layer defines the mechanical connections like the types of cable, sockets and plugs and the **network interface card**.

Physical schema This is the same as the *physical level* of a **database management system**. *It refers to the physical ways in which the* **data** *are actually stored on the disks*. It is also called the **internal schema** or **storage schema**.

Picosecond See **psec**.

Pilot scheme *This is a common technique for implementing a system in which a new system is tested, usually by one department or division within a company, before going ahead with the main system*. If the pilot scheme proves to be successful, then it can be transferred to other departments by using **direct implementation**. Pilot schemes are also a good mechanism for carrying out staff **training**, because staff can be transferred to the pilot system for training purposes only.

PIM See **Personal Information Manager**.

Pipeline architecture A **microprocessor** architecture *set up so that one instruction may be fetched at the same time as another one is being decoded at the same time another is being executed*. Therefore, three different things are literally happening in the pipeline at the same time. Sometimes the next instruction to be fetched is not the one that occurs just after the **current instruction**. In this case the pipeline will have to be flushed.

Pivot table A pivot table is a method of summarising information in tabular form using specific fields from a **database** or **spreadsheet**. Typically calculations may be carried out on the data, and the data may be displayed in alternative ways by pivoting (transposing) rows and columns to get alternative views.

Pixel-based graphic See **bit-mapped graphic**.

Pixels These are the *tiny dots that make up a picture (computer graphic)*. The name pixel is made up from PIX (the slang for pictures) and Element. On a **PC** different screen resolutions like '800 × 600', '1024 × 768' and '1280 × 1024' etc. are defined in terms of the number of pixels that can be displayed on the screen at any moment in time. The greater the resolution required and the more colours that are needed, the more memory and more processing power required, usually provided by means of a better **graphics card**.

Platform This is *the name used for certain combinations of* **hardware** *and* **operating system software**. A **PC** running **Windows**, or a Mac running **MacOS**, for example.

Plotter *This is an* **output peripheral** *device for the production of drawings, typical of those used by architects and engineers*. The plotter moves pens over a piece of paper in two dimensions under the control of a computer. The A4 and A3 plotters have been superseded by A4 and A3 **ink jet printers** and **laser printers**, but the A2, A1 and larger plotters are *still used for the production of large drawings*. The larger plotters are ideal to print out the huge drawings, like the track layouts inside of a **microprocessor**, for example. When these drawings are printed out people can literally walk over the print out checking the minute detail with a magnifying glass. Some of these plotters can be the size of a small room.

Point of Presence *This is an access point to the* **Internet**, typically used by an **ISP** and provided by telecommunication companies like BT. Typical ISPs have many points of presence enabling people to connect to the Internet for the cost of a local phone call.

Point Of Sale terminal See **POS terminal**.

Point to point tunnelling protocol This is *a* **secure protocol**, *predominantly used for* **Virtual Private Networks**. **PPTP** *allows users to access their private* **LANs** *via the* **Internet**, *thus creating a* **virtual connection** *to their* **intranet** *which is private*. The word *tunnelling* is important, because this means that a **protocol** can be encapsulated within **packets** that are sent over another **network** that uses a completely different protocol. This is how Internet users can access their LANs.

Pointer (1) This is a symbol used to point at some object on the screen. It is an integral part of a **GUI operating system**. Together with **windows**, **icons** and **menus**, these create the fundamental components of a **WIMP** environment.

Pointers (2) When setting up **data structures** like **lists**, **queues** and **trees**, it's necessary to have pointers (*numbers* or **vectors**) to help manage the way in which the structure is implemented and controlled. *Typical examples of pointers would be* **start pointers**, **end pointers**, **stack pointers**, **alphabetical pointers** or **free memory pointers**.

Polymorphism This is *a concept used in* **object-oriented programming**. *Polymorphism means 'many forms', and refers to entities behaving differently according to the context in which they are being used*. References in a **base class** may behave differently when used in a **derived class**, for example.

Pop The name given to the process of taking data off a **data structure** called a **stack**. This term should be compared with the term **push**.

POP (1) See **Point of Presence**.

POP (2) This is the Post Office Protocol used by **e-mail** systems. It is one of the **protocols** used to retrieve e-mails from a **mail server**.

Port (1) A port is another name for an **I/O port**.

Port (2) On a **network**, *this is the name given to a logical communication channel*. E.g. Port 80 is usually the **default** port used by an **Internet browser**. When using a **URL** the port number may also be specified. Also see the terms **socket** and **port number**.

Port number *A number assigned to one of the 65,536 different ports that may be associated with a particular* **IP address**. In this way, the same IP address can reference one or more **servers**, thus giving access to many more resources than would appear at first sight. *Many of these port numbers have been assigned by convention* (e.g. 80 is the default port number for **http** and 23 is the default number for **telnet**.), but *others may be assigned by the server administrator*, and given out to users so they may access additional resources. It is usual to close up as many of these ports as is practical on a **file server** to prevent **hacking**.

Portable Document Format This is a popular system, developed by Adobe, which *enables people to conveniently exchange documents* in what's called Portable Document Format or **PDF**. Acrobat reader is distributed free by Adobe on the **web**, but you will need Adobe Acrobat to produce the documents in the first place. A PDF file is the most popular way of disseminating **documentation** like 'computer manuals' or 'training material' on the web. This is because the document will look right on the screen or on the printer, irrespective of **operating system**, type of computer or the fonts installed on your computer.

POS terminal *This is a Point Of Sale terminal*. It is the name given to a typical set of **hardware** and **software** consisting of *all the equipment necessary to manage sales in a shop*. It could include a **bar code reader**, a cash register, **credit card** and **debit card** payment facilities, and usually links to the store's **minicomputer**, **mainframe computer** or networked **file server** for stock control purposes.

Post-order traversal When **traversing** a **tree data structure** using this method we visit **nodes** in the order 'Left', 'Right' and 'Root'. The term *post-order* refers to the fact that we visit the **root node** last (*post*). If the tree has **subtrees**, we make a **recursive** call to traverse the subtree using the post-order traversal mechanism again.

Postscript A **page description language** developed by Adobe.

PPTP See **point to point tunnelling protocol**.

Predicate This is a term used in **logic programming**. It forms the 'name part' of a **fact**. If the **declarative language Prolog** is used to help define two facts 'cousin(bert,charlie).' and 'female(susie).', then the names 'cousin' and 'female' are the predicates. See also **fact**, **rule** and **question**. At A2 you do not need to know the formal (logical) definition.

Pre-order traversal When traversing a **tree data structure** using this method we visit **nodes** in the order 'Root', 'Left' and 'Right'. The term *pre-order* refers to the fact that we visit the **root node** first (*pre*). If the tree has **subtrees**, we make a **recursive** call to traverse the subtree using the pre-order traversal mechanism again.

Presentation layer This is *layer six* of the **ISO OSI model**. This layer *helps to maintain compatibility between different systems of coding, file handling and* **character sets**. It may carry out these conversion processes so the transmitting and receiving machines may communicate effectively. The presentation layer links the **session layer** to the **application layer**.

Presentation package This is **software** *that is designed to help people give lectures by producing a sequence of slides and other supporting materials*. Videos, sounds, **animation** and links to **files** on an **intranet** and the **Internet** are also possible. A good example of a presentation package is Microsoft's PowerPoint.

Pretty good privacy Probably *the* most popular **strong encryption** system making use of **public keys** and **private keys**. This is widely available for free on the **Internet**. It is illegal to make use of encryption software in some countries.

Primary domain name server A **domain name server** in which the *definitive list* of **domain names** is held. Secondary domain name servers, still considered to be *authoritative*, derive their lists of domain names from the primary domain name servers.

Primary index An **index**, built up from the **data** in the **primary key field**. If a **file** or **database table** is to be processed *sequentially*, then the *primary index would determine the order* in which this processing takes place.

Primary key In a **database** or **data file**, the *unique* **key field** (or group of fields for a **composite primary key**) by which a particular **record** is identified. In a database an **index** is maintained using the primary key information, which, in the absence of other factors, determines the order in which the records will be processed.

Primary key field See **primary key** and **key field**.

Primary storage The *main (electronic) memory* (**RAM**) *used inside a computer system*. This holds the most frequently used instructions like **applications** currently being run, parts of the **operating system** currently in use and the user's **programs**. Primary storage should be contrasted with **secondary storage** devices like **disk** and **tape**.

Print out This is a **hard copy** of the results of some processing. For example, a program could produce a list of numbers in alphabetical order output to the printer. Compare with the term **program listing**.

Printer A *device used to produce* **hard copy** *on paper*. The most common types of printer are **laser printers**

and the **ink jet printers**, but **dot-matrix printers** are still used for special purposes.

Printer server A **file server**, usually on a **LAN**, *set up to control printing*, usually to a large number of **printers** for a large number of **users**. There may be a **database** on this server which monitors the amount of printing undertaken by individuals and departments, and will thus be able to audit what's going on, usually for accounting purposes.

Private This is *a concept used in* **object-oriented programming**, *as a mechanism for controlling* **inheritance**. It is a mechanism used by the **base class** to define what properties are **private**, and therefore not available to any **derived class**. Any derived class would *not* inherit any data that is private. If data is to be made available to all classes then the keyword **public** may be used. See also **class attributes**.

Private key A special key, *known only to you*, which is *used by you to decrypt messages* that other people send making use of your **public key**. Keys are actually factors of large prime numbers, and it takes enormous computing power and ridiculously long periods of time to try to work out the private key by using the public key.

Problem definition This is the part of a computer project which specifies *exactly what problem has to be solved*. It is part of the **classic system life cycle**. Without a detailed definition of the problem, people would often not know what's got to be achieved, and the problem might get solved completely out of context if this is not done effectively. The detailed definition of the problem is usually written up in a project specification. See also **objectives**.

Problem investigation This is the part of a computer project consisting of a simple analysis of the problem, including the current methods of solution (if any), together with **interviews** and **questionnaires**, deciding possible alternative solutions, and trying to make an estimate of the cost effectiveness of the solution. If a system is *not* cost effective, it should be stopped at the **feasibility study** stage.

Procedural programming Procedural programming, like **imperative programming**, typifies writing sequences of program statements to solve a problem. *It is ideal for problems which can be expressed hierarchically, usually by means of using a* **hierarchical diagram**. Most modern **high-level languages** support procedural programming, which typifies modularisation, or being able to split up the **program** into **procedures**, in which **parameter** passing may be **by value** or **by reference**. Modern procedural programming allows a team of programmers to help develop a problem by splitting the problem up into appropriate modules that can be worked on independently.

Procedure In programming, this is the name given to a **subprogram** which can receive **parameters** from the calling program, and pass parameters back to the calling program. These parameters may be passed **by value** or **by reference**. A procedure is usually called by name, and procedure definitions usually go at the beginning or the end of the main program, thus ensuring good **structured programming** style.

Process This is *the execution of a particular program from an* **operating system** *perspective*. A process may be in any one of a number of **process states**.

Process control industry Plant like nuclear power stations, chemical factories, steel works and robots *which are controlled by computers or* **embedded systems**.

Process state One of a range of states in which a particular **process** can exist. A process can be considered to be in a number of different states, examples of which may include 'waiting to run', 'awaiting peripheral attention' or 'being run'.

Processor The name given to the **CPU** or Central Processing Unit. On *larger computers* the CPU might be made up of *many* **microprocessors**, but a **PC** would normally have only one or two, housed on the **motherboard** inside the computer.

Program A *set of instructions* to control the actions of a computer. *Note the spelling of the word*. Program is used as opposed to 'Programme', which would define a 'programme of study' or a 'television programme', for example.

Program code See **program**.

Program control instructions This is a term normally associated with **assembly language**. These instructions typify sending *control* to another part of the program by performing a jump, usually to a **label**.

Program counter The *alternative name* for this is a **sequence control register**. *This determines the sequence in which an assembly program is executed, because the number stored inside this* **register** *represents the memory location from where the next* **assembly language** *instruction is to be fetched*. If a jump instruction is to be executed, then the destination for this jump would be placed in the program counter.

Program editor An *editor used for the production of* **program code**. These range from a simple **text editor** to produce the **source code** for the **compiler** or **assembler**, through to Microsoft's IDE (Integrated Development Environment) for Visual Programming (e.g. the **Visual Basic** Editor). Such *visual environments provide a set of sophisticated functions that help to develop the program from initial concept through to completion and testing*.

Program flowchart This type of **flowchart** consists of special symbols for 'start' and 'stop', 'process', 'input/output' and 'decision making' etc., which are connected together by *arrows which indicate the flow of data*. The program flowchart is useful for representing detailed **algorithms**, although the size and structure of the flowchart can become unwieldy if the algorithm being represented is complex. **Pseudocode** is often used as an alternative for representing algorithms at program-code level.

Program listing This is a **hard copy** of a program or **source code**. Compare with the term **print out.**

Program statement This is a *basic unit* describing operations and other information to be carried out in a **programming language**. Groups of program statements may be joined together to form **program structures**. Typical examples of program statements are 'IF x = 1 THEN y = 2' or 'Area = PI*radius ^ 2'. The **syntax** of the program statement depends on the language being used, but the **semantics** (*meaning*) of these statements should be unambiguous and reasonably obvious, even if you are unfamiliar with a particular **high-level language**.

Program structure Most modern **high-level languages** support *good program structure*. And **structured programming** is a desirable goal in computer science. Typical examples of program structures are 'FOR TO NEXT loops', **procedures** and **functions**, but **structured programming** also involves other techniques like using sensible **variable** names and **comments** etc.

Programmer A *person who writes computer programs*. They are usually divided into **systems programmers** and **applications programmers**.

Programming language *This is a* **high-level language** *or* **low-level language** *used to program a computer system*. There are a large variety of high-level and low-level programming languages and programming **paradigms**, all useful for solving *specific types* of problem.

Programming paradigm This is the name given to the main *method of working* or *model* that is used to solve a problem when a particular **programming language** is used. Typical programming paradigms are **object-oriented programming**, **procedural programming**, **logic programming** and **functional programming**, for example. Different paradigms make different types of problem easier to solve.

Project diary This is *a document which records the progress you have made in your A2 (or AS) project*. If the documentation is sufficiently detailed, it will help you considerably with your project write up. It will also help your teachers to monitor your progress.

Projector These are multimedia *output devices*, which can be portable or mounted on the ceiling, to produce *high-quality computer displays for large audiences*. In recent years they have become affordable for institutions like schools, thus getting over the problem of large classes not being able to view a single **computer monitor** at the front of the class. These projectors can also be used to display conventional video signals, and together with a suitable audio system, provide endless possibilities for the classroom, computer training and entertainment.

Prolog Prolog (PROgramming in LOGic) is a **fifth-generation logic programming** language. When using a language like Prolog, *we concentrate on the* **declarative** *view of the problem and are not concerned with the* **procedural programming** *elements needed to solve the problem*. This frees up the programmer, enabling him or her to build up sophisticated **knowledge base** systems *without* the need to specify **algorithms** to solve the problem in a **procedural** way. Prolog makes use of concepts like **rules**, **facts**, **objects** and **relationships** etc. to help the user of the program ask questions by interrogating the knowledge base. Prolog is used extensively for **expert systems** and **AI**.

PROM This is a *Programmable Read-Only Memory chip*. Unlike a conventional **ROM** chip, which can only be programmed by the manufacturer of the chip, *the PROM can be programmed by the end user*.

Protected See **class attributes**.

Protection This is *a concept used in* **object-oriented programming**, and is used as a mechanism for controlling **inheritance**. This mechanism is used by the **base class** to control what **data** may be inherited by a **derived class**. If data is to be made available to all classes then the keyword **public** should be used. Compare with the keywords **private** and **protected**.

Protocol A *set of agreed methods and rules, usually for communication between different computer systems, but also used for telephones, satellites and other devices*. These protocols help with **error detection**, thus ensuring the **integrity** of the transmitted **data**. Typical of these would be the **TCP/IP** protocol which is in common use on the **Internet**.

Protocol stack This is *a layer of* **protocols**, *in which the next layer builds upon the one/s below*. A typical example is the **TCP/IP protocol stack**, which is part of the **ISO OSI model**.

Prototype See **prototyping**.

Prototyping This is a *simulation of a system for development purposes*. An example might be the presentation of a **user interface** which appears to the **user** to work, but is only *pretending for the benefit of testing the opinions of users* to help design a particular interface. Prototyping should be used with caution. It could, for example, prove very expensive if the user is presented with a set of possibilities that might be difficult to carry out in practice, due to the complexity of programming that might be needed to achieve the real thing.

psec One millionth of a millionth of a second, i.e. 0.000000000001 sec.

Pseudo operations These are extra, helpful operations often used when assembling an **assembly language** program. See **directives**.

Pseudo real time This is the name given to a **real time operating system** in which the response has to be fast enough to respond to events, but not lightning fast as in a true real time system.

Pseudocode This is *code, written in an 'English-like way'*, which closely mirrors how an **algorithm** would be programmed using a real programming language. **Key words** like 'IF THEN', 'DO WHILE' and 'END WHILE' etc. are used in conjunction with *other* **program statements** like 'Test for end of file' etc. to describe the **control structures** and other code needed to solve a problem. It should be a relatively simple task for a competent **programmer** to take a pseudocode algorithm and change it into the actual code in the **high-level language** with which he or she is familiar. Pseudocode is a popular way of solving algorithms in examinations, because the

syntax of language in which a student has learnt to program is irrelevant, but the *principles* which the student has learnt are not.

Public This is *a concept used in* **object-oriented programming**, *as a mechanism for controlling* **inheritance**. It is used by the **base class** to define what properties are publicly available to any **derived class**. All classes may inherit public data, which is not just limited to derived classes. The keywords **private** and **protection** are used to determine what data can be inherited by the derived class. See also **class attributes**.

Public key The special key used by people *who send you* encrypted messages. However, only your **private key** (not owned by anyone else) can be used to decrypt these messages. Keys are actually factors of large prime numbers, and it takes enormous computing power and ridiculously long periods of time to try to work out the private key by using the public key.

Pure binary Pure binary is a **binary** number obtained by using the binary column headings '1', '2', '4' etc. with 1 being the **least significant bit** and the columns to the left increasing in multiples of two. Thus the decimal representation of the pure binary number '10101' would be '21' (16 + 4 + 1). Pure binary should be contrasted with other binary systems like **hexadecimal** and **Binary Coded Decimal**.

Push The name given to the process of putting **data** onto a **data structure** called a **stack**. This term should be compared with the term **pop**.

QBE This is an *easier way to create a query in a* **relational database**, *compared to writing it using* **SQL**. Using QBE means typing criteria for a particular query into a blank **record** presented to you by the **database software**. For example, you might be presented with a blank record in a library database having **attributes** 'ISBN', 'Title', 'Author', 'and Publisher'. You could then type in something like ' = Ray Bradley' in the author field, to find all books in the library by 'Ray Bradley'. The **syntax** would vary with the database being used.

Quality of communication See **mark scheme**.

Query This is *interrogation* of a **database** to *extract some specific information*. The *results* of the query may be laid out nicely by using a **report**. The query may be written in a language like **SQL**, or may be generated automatically by using the simpler facilities (see **QBE**) provided by some database software.

Query by example See **QBE**.

Question This is a term used in **logic programming**. An example of an explicit question might be to ask the computer if Jane is a man. The **syntax** of describing this question in a language like **Prolog** would be '?- man(jane).', to which the answer would hopefully be no, assuming that the appropriate set of **facts** had already been correctly entered into the **knowledge base**.

Questionnaire *A technique for finding out information which may be of use to a* **systems analyst** *when designing a new system*. Questionnaires may be anonymous for obtaining 'frank answers', or they may require the recipient's details to be included, in which case the analyst can follow up on good ideas or potential problems. Questionnaires are often used during the **feasibility study** phase of the **system life cycle**.

Queue A **FIFO data structure** which *mirrors a conventional queue* in real life. I.e. the first person to enter a shop would normally be the first person to be served. Contrast a **queue** (**FIFO**) with a **stack** (**LIFO**).

RAID This is an **acronym** for a Redundant Array of Independent Drives. There are several modes of operation, but it usually consists of two or more **disks** working in combination with each other to increase the reliability or the speed of access (or both) compared to that when using a single disk drive.

RAM See **Random Access Memory**.

Random access A method of accessing **data** where *any item of interest may be found without having to go through all the previous items first*. It does this by having **addresses** held within an **index** for each item of data that is stored. Main memory is random access because each location has a unique address. **Disks** are random access because each part of the disk has an address too.

Random Access Memory This is *very fast* **electronic memory** on the main **motherboard**. It is the **primary storage** facility found in a modern computer. Although rarely thought about in this way, the name derives from the fact that any location in memory may be accessed quickly without having to go through all the preceding locations, which would be the only mechanism available if **serial access** memory like **tape** were used.

RDBMS A Relational DataBase Management System. See **DBMS**.

Read Only Memory This is a storage device which is non-**volatile**. This means that the contents of the memory are *not lost* when power is removed from the system. The **BIOS** is a good example of code stored in **ROM**. The *BIOS settings* can be altered *because* they are stored in a separate **CMOS RAM** chip, which works in conjunction with the ROM.

Real This is the name given to a **data type** representing real numbers. A real number is a number that may contain both a fractional and integer part, and can take on a very large range of negative and positive values. Therefore, most numbers used every day for business, commerce and scientific work are examples of real numbers. See also the term **integer**.

Real time A general term denoting that a process is happening at a suitable rate given the scenario in which it is operating. See **real time operating system**.

Real time audio Audio data transmitted such that *no interruption occurs during the transmission of a signal*. A **guaranteed bandwidth** is needed to be able to do this, like that which is available from **ATM** networks or other similar systems.

Real time operating system This type of **operating system** is designed to *ensure that a* **task** *is completed in a set period of time*, usually with extreme reliability, and often interacting with real-world events. It is normally applied to **operating systems** where the response time must be *very fast indeed*, like those found inside an anti-missile missile launched from a battle ship, whose purpose it is to intercept an incoming hostile missile ten seconds before it blows up the ship. Under these conditions it's totally unacceptable to have run-of-the-mill **interactive operating systems** giving messages like 'Please wait while Windows is loading.' or 'Task not responding.' etc. Nevertheless, *a real time operating system is also used in other contexts, like airline ticket booking, where response time is not lightning fast, but must be reasonably quick*. The latter type of operation is thought of as **pseudo real time**.

Real time video *Video data transmitted such that no interruption occurs during the transmission of a signal*. A **guaranteed bandwidth** is needed to be able to do this, like that which is available from **ATM** networks or other similar systems.

Real time voice Voice data transmitted such that *no interruption occurs during the transmission of a signal*. A **guaranteed bandwidth** is needed to be able to do this, like that which is available from **ATM** networks or other similar systems.

Recalculation A term *usually associated with a* **spreadsheet**, but it can be applied to a variety of similar situations. If a model has been set up within a spreadsheet, then one of the main points of using a spreadsheet is to find out how variations in **data** in one part of the sheet will affect data in other parts of the sheet. When values are altered, any dependent cells will have to be recalculated to reflect the changed data.

Record A *single occurrence* representing a particular instance of an object being modelled in a **database** or **file**. A record corresponds to a row entry in a **database table**. A record is usually made up from a number of **fields**, and is identified by a **key field**. An example of a record would be the information about a particular book held in a library database.

Record locking *To prevent different users from updating the same* **record** *in a* **database** *at the same moment in time* – if one **user** is updating a particular record, then it's locked. This means *other users will be prevented from opening it for update until it is released by the first user*. Many users may read the same record, but only the first to attempt an update may be allowed to do so.

Recursion *A programming technique in which a* **procedure** *is allowed to call itself*. It is a very powerful technique that leads to concise and efficient code. Recursion is usually implemented by a **data structure** called a **stack**. Recursive **algorithms** are used extensively for **searching** and **traversing tree structures**.

Recursive call A call to a routine which makes use of **recursion**.

Recursive routine This is a routine (or program) that is allowed to call itself. The recursive calls are usually controlled by a **data structure** called a **stack**. See also the term **factorial**.

Re-entrant code *This is code that can be used by other* **programs** *and* **tasks** *simultaneously*. It is also known as **code sharing**. It is a method, usually used by the **operating system**, to ensure that the same code *does not* have to be loaded into the system a multiple number of times.

Referential integrity If a **foreign key** is referenced, updates can be cascaded. This means that multiple **tables** containing identical **fields** will be *updated automatically*.

Refinement This is a term used in **object-oriented analysis**, and describes one sort of **relationship**. A refinement is a relationship between *different descriptions of the same thing at two different stages of development*. On a **class diagram** this could indicate one class at the **analysis** stage and the same class at the **design** stage. *A refinement relationship is shown with a dotted arrow*, with the head of the arrow pointing towards the latest stage of the development. See also **object-oriented analysis** and **object analysis diagrams**.

Register An electronic circuit which stores a group of **binary digits**. Examples of registers are the **accumulator**, **program counter** and **flag register** inside a **microprocessor**.

Register addressing This is where **data** *is transferred from a* **source register** *into a* **destination register**. An example is 'mov dx, ax', where ax is the source register and dx is the destination register. This particular instruction shows data being moved from the ax register into the dx register.

Register set *The set of* **registers** *associated with a particular* **microprocessor**. Different manufacturers will use different names for the registers within a particular processor, but all registers have similar functionality, like the **accumulator** and **flag registers**, for example. The register set provides the **programmer** with a mental picture of the architecture of a particular microprocessor from an **assembly language** programming perspective.

Regulation of Investigatory Powers Act This act controls the interception and encryption of **e-mails** and other communications over public and private **networks** without lawful authority or the permission of both parties sending the communications. However, the government has given the right to employers to monitor employees' electronic communications in the work place. It is also permissible to monitor e-mails if the employees or pupils in an educational institution, for example, are using the computers for unauthorised access or are breaching the policy of the institution.

Relation A relation *is a* **relational database table** *with the following properties*. (1) It must have a unique **primary key**. (2) Each row in the table must be unique. (3) It should model only one **entity**. (4) The ways in which columns and rows are laid out is not important. (5) All the **attribute** names must be different. Don't confuse this term with a **relationship**.

Relational database A **database** in which a set of related **tables** are used to model the **data**, as opposed to one big **file**, which is called a **flat file database**.

Relational database model This is currently *the* most popular method of **database** design. The **data** is split up into **tables** or **relations**, related to each other by means of **relationships**. Each table models a particular **entity**, like a 'book' or a 'customer', for example. The columns in these tables represent the **fields** and the rows represent the **records**. Tables are usually **normalised** to ensure that the data is stored efficiently with a minimum of errors.

Relationship (1) This is a term used to show the relationships between two **relations** (tables) in a **relational database**. A relationship can be **one-to-one**, **one-to-many**, **many-to-one** or **many-to-many**. However, *only the first three of these relationships may be modelled in a relational database*. For example, a many-to-many relationship would be modelled in terms of several one-to-many relationships.

Relationship (2) This is a term used in **object-oriented analysis**. From an object-oriented analysis point of view, when developing **class diagrams**, it is useful to show relationships between **classes** by drawing annotated lines and arrows. Relationships may be categorised into **associations**, **generalisations**, **dependencies** or **refinements**. See also **object-oriented analysis**.

Relative address The *address of* a **memory** *location which is calculated by reference to some base point*. If relative addressing is used, then because of the mechanism just described, code will work wherever it is placed in the computer's **memory map**, and thus **relocatable code** is produced. It is good practice to use relative addressing and preferably not use or severely limit **absolute addressing**.

Relative path name A *path name that is relative to some particular base point*. It is used extensively when **Internet web sites** are being designed. Usually everything has a path name which is relative to the root of the site. **Absolute path names**, like 'C:\main site\department\department.htm' should *not be used* as the C drive to which it refers is unlikely to be available to those who wish to make use of this particular resource.

Relocatable code *This is code that can run anywhere in* **main memory** (i.e. the code does not have to be loaded into a specific memory location to work) and/or the code does not write to any *specific* memory location. *Most code should be relocatable, or the* **operating system** *will not be able to load it into the most appropriate place*. Problems may also arise with references pointing to the wrong place. **Relative addressing** is used to create relocatable code.

Rendering This is the production of a *2-D photo realistic image* from a 3-D modelling system. Enormous amounts of computer power are needed to render a single image in a sensible amount of time. Features such as shading, shadows, refraction and reflection are all incorporated to add realism to the computer generated image.

Repeater A device used on a **network** to *boost signals* so that they may travel over a longer distance. Typically this device may be used to extend the effective length of a **LAN** or **WAN**.

Repetitive strain injury There are injuries to the hands, back, eyes or neck etc. caused by *excessive use of a particular piece of equipment* like a **keyboard** or **games console**. Frequent breaks are suggested for **users** who do the *same activity* all day.

Report (database) A report *is the nicely formatted output from a* **database** *displaying the results of a particular* **query**. It is usual to put 'titles', 'headers', 'footers' and 'logos', and to *tabulate the output so that it is attractive and understandable*. The records displayed are usually sorted into some particular order, and statistics may be calculated and displayed.

Reserved word See **key word**.

Reset (1) A term used to *make a particular* **bit** *have a value of '0'*.

Reset (2) *A term used to start up a machine from scratch*. A *soft reset* is a reset carried out from the keyboard, a *hard reset* is a reset carried out by pressing the reset button, but the most effective reset of all may be to completely power down the machine and remove the mains for a few seconds, and then switch on again.

Resolution This is the number of points (**pixels**) used to create an image on a computer **monitor** or a **printer**, for example. Typically this would be measured in d.p.i. or dots per inch. Thus, if a printer is set to 600 d.p.i., then for every square inch the image would be made up from 600 × 600 or 360,000 dots. The higher the resolution, the better quality image is produced, but more memory is needed to produce and process the image.

Review of existing paperwork A *method used by* **systems analysts** *when gathering information during the fact finding phase of the computerisation of a new* **system**. The paperwork used in a manual system may be scrutinised to see if the methods of working are efficient, or need to be altered when the new system is designed.

RGB The red, green and blue components of colour used to make up many different colours using the **additive colour system**.

Right pointer This *concept is used in a* **binary tree data structure**. It is a *number* (or **vector**), *often stored along with the* **node** *data, which points to the right-hand* **child node**. On a tree diagram a **pointer** is represented by an arrow.

Ring topology In **network topology**, a system where all the computers on a **network** are connected to the same communications channel that forms a ring (*a continuous loop in terms on connectivity rather than a physical shape*). The **data** on the network is passed from one machine to the next, with each machine having the job of sending it on unless it's required for that machine. Compare with **token ring**.

ROM See **Read Only Memory**.

ROM BIOS See **BIOS**.

Root The top part of a **directory**, or the **root node** of a **tree structure** or **hierarchical diagram**.

Root directory The root directory is the top level or starting point for a **hierarchical directory structure**. All **files** and resources are either *contained in the root directory* or **subdirectories** of it. Each **disk** (or **partition**) on a computer would have a different root directory.

Root node The 'top' item of data in a **tree structure** i.e. the **node** from which the rest of the **tree** is derived.

Root server A root server is a **name server** that has access to the *definitive information* for the **top-level domains**, which are obtained from designated authorities which administer the **domain**. Information, held in **databases** on a limited number of root servers is used as the source of information to update the many name servers held by **ISPs** and other similar organisations. The root servers are updated from authorities like VeriSign, for example, who keep the definitive list for the '.com domain'.

Rotate This is a term normally associated with **assembly language**. This is *similar in principle to a* **shift**, *but instead of the* **bits** *'dropping off the end' of the* **register** *they* are *fed back into the other end* of the same register. There are two types of rotate instructions, called **rotate left** and **rotate right**.

Rotate left This is a term normally associated with **assembly language**. A rotate left instruction *shifts the* **bits** *left with the leftmost bit of the register being fed back into the rightmost bit*.

Rotate right This is a term normally associated with **assembly language**. A rotate right instruction *shifts the* **bits** *right with the rightmost bit of the register being fed back into the leftmost bit*.

Router In a **network**, *a* **hardware** *device that manages* **routing**. It ensures that **messages** get sent to the appropriate destination. It does this by using the **IP addresses** to split up the network into suitable **subnets**. This unit can be used for forwarding **packets** of **data** from one **LAN** to another LAN, or from a LAN to a **WAN**. It can also be used for added security, making sure that some machines never get to see data which is intended for others. Sophisticated **managed hubs** can now perform routing operations too.

Routing In a **network**, the ability to determine where **data** is to be sent, as opposed to sending it everywhere and thus using up valuable **bandwidth**. Routing is often achieved by using **IP addresses**, and is essential for large **Ethernet** networks and the **Internet** to operate effectively.

RSI See **repetitive strain injury**.

Rule This is a term used in **logic programming**. *A rule specifies conditions that must be satisfied if something is to be regarded as being true*. In **Prolog**, for example, a rule allows us to make use of many *conditional statements*. Classic examples of rules are building up family relations like 'father', 'grandfather' or 'sister'. If we wish to build up a rule to determine if 'X is a sister of Y', then the *conditions to be satisfied* would have to be 'X is female', 'X has a mother M and a father F', *AND* 'Y also has the same mother M and father F'. Therefore, using the **syntax** of Prolog, this may be written as follows

```
sister_of(X,Y) :-
   female(X),
   parents(X,M,F),
   parents(Y,M,F).
```

This defines the rule 'sister_of' as consisting of the set of facts 'X is a female', 'X has parents M and F' and 'Y has parents M and F'. *The 'conclusion part' of the rule is at the head*, being the line 'sister_of(X,Y) :-', and *the 'condition part' is the main body* (indented part) of the code.

See also **fact** and **question**.

Scanner *A device for inputting images or text into the computer* by placing them onto a flat surface similar to that of a photocopier. Images are usually scanned as a **bitmap**, and text, also scanned in as a bitmap, can be converted into computer-readable form by using suitable **OCR software**.

Scheduler This is the part of the **operating system** which arranges **scheduling**.

Scheduling This is one of the processes carried out by the **operating system** to ensure that **tasks** are carried out in a suitable order. It is the job of the **scheduler** to make sure that no one **process** hogs all the attention, or fails to get attention, and that the peripherals are used in an efficient way. The operating system copes by considering each process to be in a variety of **states**.

Schema The schema is basically *a description of the database for use in a* **relational database management system**. A DBMS is usually split up into three different schemas, namely the **users' schema**, the **conceptual schema** and **physical schema**.

Screen shot A picture taken of the computer screen, usually with the intention of including it in a project report write up such as the one you have to do for your **A2** or **AS project**. It is usually achieved by copying the screen contents to the clipboard, or using an **art package** like PaintShop Pro to capture part or all of the screen under certain conditions (like a time delay or the press of a special button). Extra annotation may be added to your screen shots by loading them into an art package or by using a **word processor**.

Scripting language This is a relatively simple **programming language** designed to perform specialist tasks such as linking a **database** to a **web site**. This could be achieved by using **Active Server Page** scripts to create dynamic web content. Another example is making a fancy interface for a **web browser** using **JavaScript**.

Scripts This is a **program**, written in a special-purpose language, like a **macro language** or **JavaScript**. Such scripts enable the **user** to perform a sequence of pre-programmed operations in the case of a macro language, or to provide some added functionality not available from a normal **web page**, in the case of JavaScript.

Search algorithm An **algorithm** for *finding a particular item of* **data** *from a list of data*, or finding out that the item of data is not in the list. Typical examples are a **linear search** or a **binary search**. See **searching**.

Search engine *A term used to describe the* **software** *and methods to search for items of* **data**, *usually on the* **Internet** *or an* **intranet**. Search engines are built up by using a variety of methods including sending **bots** or **spiders** round the **web** to gather their own information, or by searching other search engines and correlating the results (eliminating duplicates).

Searching This means *looking for a particular item of* **data** *in a list*. There are two search **algorithms** needed for A2 level, and these are the **linear search** and the **binary search**.

Second-generation language *The second generation of computer programming language is* **assembly language**. This language makes use of **mnemonics**, and is a great improvement over using **machine code**.

Second normal form *This is one of the rules carried out to ensure errors are minimised when designing a* **relational database**. This rule states that *all* **attributes** *in an* **entity** *are* **functionally dependent** *(depend only) upon the* **primary key** *or* **composite primary key**. You should remember that **data** must already be in **first normal form** *before* attempting to put it into second normal form. See also **first normal form**, **third normal form** and **BCNF**.

Secondary index *An index, built up from the* **data** *in a* **secondary key field**. If a **file** or **database table** is to be searched for information other than that contained in the **primary key field**, then a **secondary index** will help to speed up this process.

Secondary key See **secondary key field**.

Secondary key field A **field** within a **file** or **database**, other than the **key field**, on which another **index** is built. This index is used to quickly locate information within a file or database on criteria other than that contained within the key field. For a library database, books could have a **primary key** of 'ISBN number', but a **secondary key** of 'Title'. Any field can be indexed, but the overheads of doing so are a trade off between the frequency of use of a particular index and the speed with which it is acceptable to find the given information.

Secondary storage Storage devices such as **floppy disks**, **hard disks**, **zip disks** or **tape**. Such devices are non-**volatile**, and thus do not lose their contents when power is removed from the system. This term should be compared with **primary storage**.

Secure link A link *in which the* **data** *transmitted and received is kept secret*, usually by means of using **encryption**.

Secure port **Ports** *may be made secure such that unauthorised access to them is not possible*. This is usually based on certain criteria, like the **MAC address** (a special number used to identify a particular machine attempting connection) being blocked or allowed, for example.

Secure sockets layer This is a **protocol** *for sending documents securely across the* **Internet** *by means of* **encryption**. Your **private key** is used to encrypt the **data** and your **public key** is used to decrypt it. SSL is designed to set up a secure connection between the **client machine** and the **web server**. It is often used when **credit card**, **debit card** and other confidential information is transmitted. You should contrast this with **https**, which is designed to protect individual messages used from a **browser** running an **html** page.

Secure web browser A **web browser** *that is running a secure* **protocol** *like* **https**, for example. If using Microsoft's Internet Explorer browser, a secure link is confirmed by the display of a small padlock in the bottom right hand side of the browser window.

Security See **data security**.

Segment The name given to *a portion of a network in which traffic intended for this portion goes to no other parts of the network.* It is also known as a **subnet**, and is helpful in managing network **bandwidth**. Also see **network segment**.

SELECT This *term is used when producing a* **query** *in a* **relational database**. The **key word** 'Select' is used to *select* **data** when using **SQL**. See the other SQL key words '**From**' and '**Where**'.

Selection statement In a **programming language**, a *selection statement is one that makes a choice depending on the value of some particular* **variable**. 'If x = 300 then y = 2' would be an example of a selection statement, which tests the value of x, and puts y = 2 if the value of x is equal to 300. The value of y would not be altered if x were any other value.

Semantics Semantics is the *meaning applied to a particular language*, as opposed to the **syntax** of its definition. The *meaning* of a language depends on the *context* in which it is being used. Natural languages like English and German are context sensitive languages, but formal languages, like 'computing languages' are not. Computing languages must obey the strict rules of syntax. At A2 level you do not need to know the formal definition of semantics applied to computer languages.

Sensors These are **input devices** which are normally used in conjunction with **data loggers**. *Sensors convert physical quantities* like temperature, pH or pressure *into an electrical signal* (usually an **analogue signal**) which is then fed into the data logger before being changed (by an **ADC**) into a **digital signal** ready to be processed by the computer.

Sequence control register See **program counter**.

Sequential access file An **ordered file** in which the **records** *are stored one after the other in some predetermined sequence like alphabetical order, for example.* All previous **data** items must be gone through before the item of interest can be found, or found not to be in the **file**. *Once found, the rest of the file does not have to be searched.* This is typical of the file structure used for **tape** storage, but it can also be implemented on **disk**, especially if the file needs to be processed in a **batch operation**. This method is slow compared to using **random access** methods like disks or **RAM**. Compare this with a **serial access file** and a **random access file**.

Serial access file A **data file** *in which* **records** *are stored one after the other with no regard to any particular order.* This is typical of a **transaction file** that would be created during a typical day in a retail business. Compare with a **sequential access file** and a **random access file**.

Serial data communication This is a data communication channel in which single **bits** (**binary** digits) of **data** are *transmitted one after the other.* This form of transmission *is ideal when only one line of communication is available*, like that found in a **network**, telephone system or wireless link. The *rate at which the data is transmitted is important*, or else it will be misinterpreted when it is received. **Start bits** and **stop bits** ensure that the appropriate synchronisation can take place. Compare with **parallel data communication**.

Serial port A serial interface designed to transfer a stream of **binary digits** *one bit after another* to some serial device like a **modem**, for example.

Server farm This is *a group of* **file servers** *working together*, usually as a source of **programs** and **data** on an **intranet** or the **Internet**.

Session layer This is *layer five* of the **ISO OSI model**. *It is the job of the session layer to manage logging on and logging off, and for establishing and terminating connections.* The session layer links the **transport layer** to the **presentation layer**.

Set A term used to set a particular **bit** to have a value of '1'.

Sexual Offences Act This act is designed to protect children and the vulnerable. The important point from a computing perspective is that it is now an offence to groom children by using the **Internet**. People often masquerade as other people when using chat rooms (see **Internet relay chat**).

Shift This is *a term normally associated with* **assembly language**. It is a **logical operation** in which the bit pattern inside a **register** gets shifted (moved along) either left or right. There are two different types of shift; an **arithmetical shift** and a **logical shift**.

Shopping bot An **agent** set up specifically to help find bargains when shopping on the **Internet**. It is ideal for researching into the price and performance of goods, or for comparing different makes of electronic or white goods, for example.

Shrink wrapped software **Software** *that is 'shrink wrapped' and sold in shops like computer stores, supermarkets or ordered via the* **web**. It is usually accompanied by minimal **documentation**, and **users** *can expect little or no support from the manufacturers, other than telephone help lines.* Software like 'Office Suites', 'Games', 'Tax Calculators' and 'CAL packages' are typical of this type of software.

Sign and magnitude A simple system of representing both positive and negative **binary** numbers in which the **most significant bit** represents the sign bit; which is 0 for positive numbers and 1 for negative numbers. The remainder of the digits are treated as a pure binary number. Thus 0001 would be +1 and 1001 would be −1. This term should be compared with **two's complement** notation.

Sign bit A binary digit that is used to denote the sign of a binary number. It is a '0' for positive numbers and a '1' for negative numbers in both the **sign and magnitude** and **two's complement** notation.

Simple Mail Transfer Protocol SMTP is *the normal* **protocol** *for sending* **e-mail** *over the* **Internet**. Some parts of the Internet still rely on systems that use only **ASCII codes**, and thus any **binary files** that need to be transferred over the Internet by e-mail must be **encoded** into this form. **MIME encoding** is the system used to carry out this process in practice.

Sister node A **node** *having other nodes on the same level in a* **subtree**. (Same as a **brother node**.) A brother or sister node *must* share the same **parent node**.

Smart board See **interactive white board**.

Smart card This is *a card, like a* **credit card**, *with* a *small microchip inside it*. The chip is capable of storing a variety of information, which is capable of being read by a smart-card reader. Smart cards are ideal for 'ID cards', 'medical cards', as a 'replacement for cash' or for 'key replacement' in hotel rooms etc. Some smart cards have a **microprocessor** inside them, but others *have only the capacity to store* **data**, which is processed by a microprocessor in the smart card reader.

SMTP See **Simple Mail Transfer Protocol**.

Socket This is a way of *connecting data to a particular application. The* **URL**, *(or* **IP** *address) in combination with a* **port number** *represents a socket*, and is therefore able to direct data. As an example, using port number 1234, the URL http://www.myweb.com:1234/path/subdirectory/top/secret.doc would link you to the 'topsecret.doc' file, *not available through the standard socket* which uses **port** 80 by default. If you were to type 'http://www.myweb.com/path/subdirectory/topsecret.doc', then this would *not find the file*, because it assumes the default of http:// www.myweb.com:80/path/subdirectory/topsecret.doc, which is the *wrong socket*. Thousands of sockets are defined for special purposes, with port numbers like 20 and 21 being used for **ftp**, for example.

Soft copy **Data** *displayed on a* **VDU** *or computer screen*. This should be contrasted with **hard copy**, which is data printed out on a printer.

Software *The* **programs** *designed to run on the computer*. Software is usually subdivided into **applications software** and **systems software**. Software should be contrasted with **hardware**.

Software drivers *Extra* **software** *needed to interface things like* **network cards**, **graphics cards** and **printers** etc. to a particular **operating system**. Without these drivers these devices would not work very well, or not work at all. Drivers are sometimes updated, and you should check on the **Internet** to make sure you have the latest version. This ensures that your computer should operate more effectively.

Software package This is a general name for **system software, application software** and **bespoke software**. This term would usually be used in the context of a particular software package, like a **CAD package**, music composition package or **authoring package**, for example.

Son file An original master file is called the **son file** which is used with the first **transaction file** to create a new master file (called the **father file**). Three generations of file are usually kept, being the **grandfather**, **father** and **son** files. This provides additional data security in the event of errors being subsequently discovered.

Sorting This refers to *putting* **data** *into some pre-determined order* like 'reverse alphabetical' or 'ascending numerical' for example. Many different **sorting algorithms** are available to do this.

Sorting algorithm This is an **algorithm** *to sort* **data** *into some specific order*, like 'alphabetical' or 'numerical ascending', for example. Typical examples would be the **insertion sort** and the **bubble sort**, *and these are the only two that are required at A2 level*.

Sound card A **daughter board** *plugged in to the main* **motherboard** *that handles sound*. Some motherboards have sound capability already built in, but if you want something more sophisticated, like Dolby 5.1 or 7.1 surround sound, then you will probably need an extra sound card to handle these features.

Sound synthesis This is the generation of sounds (musical and others) by the computer. Typically **software** might be used in conjunction with a **sound card** to synthesise sounds of musical instruments like pianos, violins and percussion. The fidelity of the sound depends upon the quality of the systems available on the sound card and on the complexity of the software being used to synthesise the sound.

Source A place from where *the* **data** *to be used in a particular process may be obtained*. This is typically used when considering **operands** in **assembly language** programming.

Source code The original **high-level language** code *before* being put through a **compiler** or **interpreter** or the **assembly language** code before being **assembled**. It is the code that the **programmer** would normally type into a suitable **editor** for the computer language they are currently using. A print out from the editor would produce a *source code listing*.

Special purpose application software This is **application software** *used by specialists*, such as high end **CAD packages**, 'music composition software' or a 'PIC programming interface' (a system for programming chips to perform a variety of functions normally carried out by lots of dedicated electronic chips soldered onto a circuit board). This term should be contrasted with **general purpose application software**.

Special purpose register **Registers** may be **general purpose** or **special purpose**. *A special purpose register is a register which is assigned a specific function, and therefore the register can't be used for* *anything else*. Examples of special purpose registers would be the **flag register** and the **accumulator**.

Specialisation This is a term used in **object-oriented analysis**. It is an alternative approach to modelling **inheritance** by **generalisation**. Specialisation involves splitting up a **class** into **subclasses** by identifying which **objects** have their own special characteristics.

Specialist agent An **agent** set up for a specialist purpose like 'shopping', or 'a specialist search', for example. However, *specialist agents can be very sophisticated autonomous pieces of* **software**. See **agent**.

Speech input This is *using the human voice to get* **data** *into or to control the computer*. Speech recognition is now quite advanced, although not yet perfect. It is easy to get spoken commands to control every aspect of the computer's **GUI interface**, by speaking the **menu**-driven commands. It's also possible to speak the words into a **word processor**, **spreadsheet** or **database**, for example. This is now a realistic form of computer input for those who have a disability, or for those who do not want to use the **keyboard** or **mouse** as the main input mechanism. Some types of job may require data to be input while both hands are engaged in doing something else, for example.

Spider See **bot**.

Spreadsheet *This is* **application software** *consisting of a tabular arrangement of cells into which numbers, text and related formulae can be typed*. Cells may be related to other cells, such that calculations performed on one cell may affect many others. If the value in a cell alters then related cells are **recalculated** to reflect this change. The analysis potential of a modern spreadsheet is extremely powerful and complex **what if scenarios** may be undertaken.

Spyware This is **software**, often deliberately installed on your computer by companies who run or advertise on **web sites** that you have visited. Information about your surfing habits may then be sent back to the company to provide them with useful statistics. You can prevent spyware from being installed by using suitable **Internet security software**.

SQL See **Structured Query Language**.

SQL database This is a **database** *built up, interrogated and queried by using the* **SQL** *language*.

SQL server This is the name of *the* **file server** *on which an* **SQL database** *is run*. Typically an SQL system would run an **RDBMS** in a **client server** configuration. All the functionality of a **Database Management System** is usually available from an SQL server.

SSL See **secure sockets layer**.

Stack A **data structure** in which the *last data item to be entered* into the structure is the *first data item to be processed*. It is also known as a **LIFO stack**. Such data structures are useful for **recursive algorithms** and processing **interrupts** in an **operating system**, for example. A stack is also useful for reversing the data elements in a list.

Stack pointer The name given to a **pointer** (*number* or **vector**) *which points to the top of a* **stack** *or* **LIFO data structure**.

Staff training This is *making sure that personnel who will make use of a system know the most efficient ways of using the system*. Staff training can be carried out by a variety of methods from 'reading manuals', 'using interactive **CD-ROMs**', 'videos', 'doing an on-line course', 'attending lectures' and 'residential courses'.

Stand alone computer This is a computer that is operating *without being connected to a* **network**.

Star topology In **network topology**, a system where all the computers are connected to a central point or central resource. On some systems this means a unique communications channel for each computer, and if set up like this, it would ensure that **data** intended for one computer never passes any other, and hence the **security** is very high. This system is sometimes used on **mainframe computers** and **minicomputers**. However, the term is also applied to computers connected to a central switch or **hub** on an **Ethernet** network. Using this configuration with an ordinary hub would *not* give any increased security.

Start bit *A* **bit** *that is used to indicate the start of transmission of some* **data**. It is usual to have a defined level (like one), when no transmission is taking place, and thus a transition from one to zero could let the receiving electronics know that some data is coming. The data must then be *clocked in at the appropriate rate* to be interpreted correctly. See also **stop bit**, **bit rate** and **baud rate**.

Start pointer This is a *number* (**vector**) used to point to the *beginning* of a **data structure** like a **FIFO structure** or **LIFO structure**. A start pointer is usually represented on a diagram with a number (representing the location to which you are pointing) and an arrow.

State This refers to one of several states that a task might be in regarding an **operating system scheduler**. Typical states might be 'Program is ready to run', 'Program is running' or 'Program is waiting for a peripheral'.

Statement See **program statement**.

Static RAM This is a form of **RAM** that does *not* need refreshing. It is usually faster than **dynamic RAM** or **DRAM**, and is often used for **cache** memory. Static RAM is still **volatile**.

Stop bit *A* **bit** *that is used to indicate the end of* **data** *being transmitted*. The stop bit would return the signal back to the original level (a **binary** one, for example), indicating to the receiving electronics that no further valid data is present. The electronics would then wait until the next **start bit** occurred to receive the next block of data. Start and stop bits are used in **asynchronous** data transmission systems. See also **start bit**, **bit rate** and **baud rate**.

Storage schema See **physical schema**.

Stored program concept This is the concept of fetching and executing a **program**, one instruction after another, but *stored inside the computer's* **main memory**. This means that the programs and **data** can be easily modified or quickly replaced by other programs and data. The stored program concept was invented by von-Neumann, a Hungarian who was living in America at the time. Virtually all computers operate on this principle.

String *A* **data type** *that can hold a string of characters. Alphanumeric characters*, contained in strings, should be contrasted with **numeric data types** which hold numbers on which arithmetical operations may be carried out. If '2' + '2' is evaluated using a string variable, then the answer would be '22'.

Strong encryption The longer the cryptographic key used for the encryption method, the more time is needed to try to break the code by guesswork alone. *Very long keys (like the 128-bit keys in current use) are regarded as strong encryption*, as opposed to **weak encryption** which can be cracked if you have enough supercomputing power. As **supercomputers** get faster, the number of **bits** needed for strong encryption may need to grow, but at the moment it would take longer than the Universe has been in existence for a supercomputer to work through all the possible codes (128-bit keys) by guessing alone, even working at speeds in excess of 1000 million guesses each second.

Structure chart See **structure diagram**.

Structure diagram *A* **hierarchical diagram** *or* **tree diagram** *which gives a visual representation of the structure of a* **program** *or* **algorithm**. The aim is to split up the program into defined modules so that different **subprograms** may be used to implement different parts. Each subprogram may be further split up into other subprograms, and this is indicated by the next level on the structure diagram. These diagrams looks a little like an upside-down version of a family tree.

Structured high-level language *Not so much a* **programming paradigm**, *but more a method of working with a* **high-level language** *that supports features like* '**functions**', '**procedures**', '**recursion**', 'a rich variety of **data types**', 'allows **constant** and **variable declaration**', 'a rich selection of **loop structures** and **control structures**', '**meaningful variable names**', '**comments**' and a whole host of other desirable attributes. It's more difficult to understand this concept than it used to be, because most **high-level languages** are now well structured.

Structured programming *The goal of structured programming is to make* **programs** *easier to understand, and thus easier to modify at a later date.* See **structured high-level language**.

Structured Query Language This is *the language used for the 'creation', 'manipulation' and 'querying' of* **relational database systems**. SQL is a structured query language, and is often pronounced as *sequel*. SQL is one of the most powerful database languages, and powerful **SQL servers** run systems like the GOOGLE search engine used on the **world wide web**, for example.

Subclass This is a term used in **object-oriented analysis**. This is a **class** which inherits properties from another class by the mechanism of **inheritance**. Therefore, if class Y inherits properties from class X, then class Y is a subclass. Compare with the term **superclass**.

Subdirectory A **directory** that is *not* a parent directory, i.e. it is held within another directory or **folder**.

Subnet The name given to a **network** which is part of a larger network. Also see **subnet mask**.

Subnet mask This is the name for an **address mask**, used to extract (or block out) information from the **IP address**. It is usual to represent all the computers in a single department or building as being a sub-network of the main network on a campus. Typically this is achieved by masking out all machines other than those for a particular department by 'placing a binary 1 where you need to look' and 'a binary zero where you need to mask'. **Routers** then use this mask information to route the **packets** more quickly. To mask off the last **byte** in an IP number the mask 255.255.255.0 could be used.

Subprogram *A self-contained program which carries out some defined* **task**, *and is usually called from another program*. Examples of subprograms are **subroutines**, **procedures** and **functions**. The ability of a programming language to be able to call a subprogram by name is fundamental to good **structured programming** techniques.

Subroutine *This is set of instructions for solving part (a subsection) of a larger problem*. It can be called by name, and is the simplest **subprogram** structure. When program statements within the subroutine have been executed, control is then passed back to the main calling routine. The name is also *informally* used to represent both **subroutines** and **procedures**. Don't confuse Visual Basic's 'Sub' and 'End Sub' **program statements** with a subroutine, because it is really a subprocedure; i.e. a proper **procedure** and *not* just a simple subroutine, which can't pass **parameters** like a procedure can.

Subscripted variable A **variable** which is used to represent elements within an **array**. Examples of using subscripted variables are A(5) for a single-dimension array or B(23,12,7) for a three-dimensional array.

Subtractive primary colours This is the **CMYK** (Cyan, Magenta, Yellow and Key (Black)) system used to *produce colours on the printed page*. The mechanism for viewing coloured print is different from viewing a colour monitor, because white light is reflected back to the eye of the user from the ink on the page. Some of the colours of the 'white' (daylight) light are absorbed (subtracted), but others are reflected, and this is what you see. *You should compare this mechanism* with the **additive colour system** used in monitors.

Subtree *A part of a* **tree structure** *which has its own* **root node** *and* **child**/(children) **nodes**.

Superclass This is a term used in **object-oriented analysis**. This is a **class** from which other classes (**subclasses**) may inherit properties by the mechanism of **inheritance**. Therefore, if class Y inherits properties from class X, then class X is a superclass. Compare with the term **subclass**.

Supercomputer A *very fast* and *extremely powerful* computer, often with hundreds or even thousands of **microprocessors** (acting together to form the **CPU**), and huge amounts of **memory**. It is ideal for forecasting the weather or other similarly intensive mathematical, scientific or engineering tasks. Typical of modern supercomputers are those designed by Silicon Graphics Inc. (formerly Cray Research Inc.).

Switch This is *a device on a network that enables two computers to communicate with each other without interfering with the* **bandwidth** *used by others*, as would be the case with a **hub**. Thus, the switch enables the full bandwidth to be maintained between the communicating computers.

Switched Ethernet An **Ethernet network** in which **segments** or computers are connected to each other by means of an **Ethernet switch**. Ethernet switches enable the full **bandwidth** to be maintained between communicating computers, assuming, of course, that the bandwidth into and out of the switch is sufficient to be able to do this.

Switching In a **network**, connecting two computers such that they are able to communicate with each other using a temporary rather than a permanent connection. We can thus **route** or *switch information very effectively without having to have hundreds of dedicated permanent connections to each computer*. It's a little like the telephone exchange, which also uses temporary connections for the duration of a phone call. Switching is used extensively in **message switching** and **packet switching** networks to establish suitable connections for the duration of the **packet** or **message**.

Symbolic In a **programming language**, *symbolic* means the *use of symbols* to represent **variables** and **key words** in the language. **BASIC** is a good example of this, where the name stands for Beginner's All-purpose Symbolic Instruction Code.

Symbolic addressing This is the use of *labels* (groups of symbols) *to represent the place in a* **program** *to which you may jump*. It is often used in **assembly language** programming, where **relative addresses** can be calculated by reference to the position at which the label is inserted in the program. Without symbolic addressing these relative jumps would have to be calculated by hand and this would be a tedious and time consuming business.

Synchronous This means that *two events are synchronised in time*. Good examples of synchronous events are the events that happen on the **motherboard** inside a computer under the control of the **clock**. This term should be compared with **asynchronous**.

Synchronous data transmission This is transmission of **data** where *the transmitting and receiving ends are synchronised*, usually by means of a **clock**. This method of transmission is suitable only for use over short distances, like those found inside a computer or close **peripheral devices** like local **printers** and **disks** etc.

Syntax **Syntax** *is the grammar of a language*, i.e. *the rules governing how a particular language is to be used*. Each **program statement** in a particular language must obey the correct syntax or a **syntax error** will occur. Syntax should be compared with **semantics**, which is the meaning applied to a language.

Syntax error An *error in the syntax* (grammatical construction) *of the language*, e.g. misspelling the keyword 'Print' as 'Pint'. Syntax errors are usually picked up by the **assembler** (for an **assembly language** program) or by the **compiler** or **interpreter** (for a **high-level language** program).

System The name given to the *entire* computer system. It is also used when **systems analysts** analyse and design the entire system including **hardware**, **software**, methods (e.g. paper-based methods etc.) and personnel.

System flowchart This is an *extension* of the **program flowchart**. However, unlike a program flowchart, the system flowchart is more useful for the **analysis** of a **system**, with many extra symbols for representing '**disks**', '**tape**', 'paper-based input/output', 'VDUs' and 'keyboards' etc. *The system flowchart is more useful to analyse a system at a macroscopic level*, whereas the *program flowchart is useful at a microscopic* (lines of code) *level*.

System life cycle This is the classic way of conducting a computer project from its conception to its conclusion. Various differences exist between systems used by different companies or personnel. However, the cycle essentially consists of subsections like '**problem definition**', '**problem investigation**', '**feasibility study**', '**information collection**', '**analysis**', '**design**', '**implementation**', '**evaluation**' and '**maintenance**'. These formalised methods, together with suitable **documentation**, are needed to help organise large teams of people in industry, and to make sure that a project comes to a successful conclusion.

System maintenance (1) See **maintenance**.

System maintenance (2) *This is a part of the documentation for your* **A2 project**. *Its purpose is to enable other people (or even you) to maintain the project at a much later stage*. Maintenance involves curing **bugs** in the project after it has been in use for some time or modification of the system if the needs of the **users** change. It is usually the case that the **documentation** for the **design** and **technical solution** sections are sufficient to satisfy the system maintenance requirements too, but don't leave the system maintenance out, refer to the other sections in a few short paragraphs entitled 'system maintenance'.

System software This is **software**, directly *used by the computer rather than the* **user**. The computer uses this software for its own 'housekeeping functions' or for running **applications**. **Operating systems**, the software contained within the **BIOS** chip and **software drivers** would all be examples of system software. It should be contrasted with **applications software**.

System specification This is *a detailed list of what a system has to do*. It is often long and complex. It is this specification that the designers of the system will use to develop the **hardware** and **software** used to implement the system. The specification is therefore tremendously important. If the specification is not correct, or contains omissions, then it's often a long and hard job to put things right at a later stage.

System testing (1) See **integration testing**.

System testing (2) This is the part of your **A2 project** where you implement the **test strategy** that you devised in the **design phase** of your project. It may involve a variety of methods, using **normal data**, **extreme data** and **erroneous data**, and involve **black box testing** or even **white box testing** techniques.

Systems analysis *This is a general term for analysing a system with the idea of producing a design specification, looking at the feasibility and the potential costs etc*. A variety of analysis methods exist, depending on the type of problem. **Object-oriented analysis** would be typical for the analysis and design of a system for solution using **object-oriented programming**. Other techniques, like **top-down design**, would be ideal for a **procedural programming** solution.

Systems analyst *A person who looks at the way in which computers can be used to solve complex problems*. This person must have an intimate knowledge of the business before attempting to suggest ways in which computers might be used to improve things. Given that a suitable **feasibility study** had been carried out, the systems analyst would then research different ways in which the problem could be solved, and come up with the most cost-effective solution that satisfies all the criteria from the project specification.

Systems programmer *A person who writes* **systems programs** *like creating parts of an* **operating system** or writing **device drivers** for a particular **graphics card**, for example.

Table A **file** in a **database**, made up of *rows* which represent the **records** and *columns* which represent the **fields**. A **relational database** is made up of two or more tables which are related. An alternative name for a table in a relational database is a **relation**. It's important to realise that tables *must conform to certain rules* (see **relation**).

Tail This is the name given to all the elements that remain in a **list** after the first item (the **head**) has been taken away. This concept is used when dealing with lists in a language like **Prolog**.

Tape This is a **serial-access** medium, ideal for **backup** of data and for **archive** purposes. A variety of forms are in common use, including **DAT** and **DLT**. It is *particularly useful for backing up work* on **network file servers**. Huge tape libraries are often found on **mainframe computers**.

Task A **program** that is *running independently of others*. If a **word processor**, **spreadsheet** and communication program are running on the computer, then these are *separate tasks*. However, the **operating system** handles many more tasks than the obvious ones mentioned here, most running without the knowledge of the **user**.

Tbyte See **terabyte**.

TCP See **Transmission Control Protocol**.

TCP/IP TCP/IP stands for **Transmission Control Protocol** *over* **Internet Protocol**. *This group of* **protocols** (**Transmission Control Protocol/Internet Protocol**) *is the most common for computer communications making use of the* **Internet**, *private* **intranets** *and* **LANs** *like* **Ethernet**.

TCP/IP protocol See **TCP/IP**.

TCP/IP stack TCP corresponds to the **transport layer** of the **ISO OSI model**, and thus has the job of assembling the **packets** into the right order. The **IP protocol** corresponds to the **network layer** of the ISO OSI model, and thus has the job of routing the data. The **stack** refers to the layered system (i.e. **TCP** on top of **IP**) used in the ISO OSI model.

TDM See **time division multiplexing**.

Technical documentation This is *the documentation that provides advanced technical* **users** *with the information they need to run, maintain and modify the system*. Technical documentation might include the **system specifications**, the design of the system, diagrams like **hierarchical diagrams** and **systems flowcharts**, **pseudocode**, program listings, detailed **file** and **data** specifications, modifications made to the system (with dates and authors etc.), **test data** with results, and information to help with **system maintenance**.

Technical help line This is *a phone line to provide help for technical problems with specific* **software**. **Users** are often charged for this service, and the level of expertise varies enormously. When competent technical personnel ask pertinent questions from experts on the other end of a phone line then the system works well. When inexperienced users ask questions, and technical personnel go through pre-set sequences of instructions then it's often fraught with difficulty and much frustration.

Technical solution This is the phase of your **A2 project** in which you implement the system on the computer. It involves using a **programming language** like **Visual Basic**, **Pascal** or **C++**, for example, or an **application package** like a **database**, or a combination of these methods. There should be **annotated listings** of any **programs** or **macros**, **screen shots** of the project in action, and output of **reports** from a **database** if this is involved in your solution. *You should never start the technical solution before carrying out the* **analysis** *and* **design** *phases*.

Telnet This is *a* **protocol** *used for remote login*. Telnet basically involves using a **terminal emulation program** to remotely control another computer connected to a **LAN** or a **WAN**. Via telnet, you can log in to the remote computer and manage it as though you were sitting at the local machine. **Web servers** are often managed remotely by making use of telnet.

Telnet console The *software which runs on a machine enabling you to remotely control other machines* (you obviously need permissions via login and password to do this) *from your machine by running* **telnet**.

Terabyte A terabyte = 1024 × 1024 × 1024 × 1024 = 1,099,511,627,776 **bytes** of **data**.

Terminal The name often given to a *dumb* **workstation** that could be connected to a **minicomputer** or **mainframe computer**, or to a **thin client** machine operating over a **network**. Conventional PCs may also be referred to as a terminal if connected to a suitable **network**, and are running **terminal emulation software**.

Terminal emulation program This is a **program** that enables you to act as though you were connected to the host computer. A typical example of a terminal emulation program is **Telnet**, which can be used for remote administration.

Terminal node The last **node** in a **tree structure** which *has no children*. This is the same as a **leaf node**.

Test data This is *dummy* **data** *used to test the system under normal, erroneous and extreme conditions*.

Ordinary data should produce results that can be verified. Abnormal data should be tested, which is expected to generate errors, and extreme data should test the limits of the **hardware** and/or **software** being used. Test data is used in combination with **black box testing** and **white box testing** methods. See also **normal data**, **erroneous data** and **extreme data**.

Test strategy This is a vital part of your **A2 project design**, in which you outline exactly how you will test your system. *It does not involve carrying out the actual tests*, but thinking up the testing methods (such as **unit testing** and **integration testing**), deciding on the **test data** to use, and coming up with examples of **normal data**, **erroneous data** and **extreme data** to be used in the tests that will be carried out during the **system testing** phase of your A2 project.

Testing This is *checking that a system works properly*. It is usually split up into **integration testing** and **module testing**.

Text editor This is an extremely simple **word processor** used to create simple text documents or **source code** for **programs**. A good example of a simple text editor is Microsoft's Notepad. See also **program editor**.

Text file *A text file is a file that contains only the characters that make up text and punctuation* (32 to 126 inclusive if **ASCII** coding is used) and special characters like 'Carriage Returns', 'Line Feeds' and 'end of file markers'. It contains no formatting information, but some text editors, like Microsoft's Notepad, for example, allow TABs to be used. Because a text file is usually made up of ASCII characters only, it is sometimes known as an **ASCII file**.

Thin client *A 'thin client' is the name given to a* **machine** *that has little local processing power and no local* **hard disks**. If you *removed the thin client computer from a* **network** *connected to a suitable* **file server**, *it could not function as a computer*. The **operating system** and other **software** like **applications** are run from a file server. The thin client acts as a **terminal** which sends streams of **data** backwards and forwards to the file server for processing. A thin client is usually used because maintenance *of the system is much easier compared to using a* **fat client**. However, thin clients are not suitable for running high-powered software requiring a lot of processing power, like '**video editing**' or 'rendering a **graphics** image', for example.

Third-generation language *Third-generation computer programming languages are the* **imperative high-level languages**. Imperative languages should be compared to a **declarative language** like **Prolog**. Whichever high-level language is used, don't forget that each high-level program **statement** gets translated into one or more **machine code** instructions. Don't forget also that machine code *is the only code that will run on any* **machine** *without* **translation**. See also **first-generation language**, **second-generation language**, **fourth-generation language** and **fifth-generation language**.

Third normal form This is *one of the rules carried out to ensure errors are minimised when designing a* **relational database**. This rule states that *there should be no* **functional dependencies** (*unique associations*) existing between **attributes** (*or groups of attributes*) that could not be used as an *alternative* to the **primary key**. You should remember that **data** must already be in **second normal form** before attempting to put it into third normal form. See also **first normal form**, **second normal form** and **BCNF**.

Third party The name given to a *company* or *individual* who *provides a service* for another company or customer. This is often used in the context of providing **utilities** or small **programs** which may be added onto an **application** or a **programming language**. A good example of this would be third party **macros** to help extend the functionality of a **word processor**. Third-party routines might save the programmer from having to re-invent code for common operations or for linking to a specific piece of **hardware** or **software**.

Threads A *thread is part of some* (usually larger) **process** *being run*. A **multithreading** system is typical of a modern **operating system**, which is able to run different parts of the same process simultaneously. See **multithreading**.

Time division multiplexing This is a method of sending *different signals* over the *same* communications link at *different moments in time*. Tiny slices of time are usually made available for each signal. The signals are given turns in using the system, (called a time slice) and if the system is very fast, all the signals *seem* to have a permanent connection.

Time sharing system This is a mode of operation where *fixed amounts of time are allocated to each* task, and a **time sharing operating system** ensures that each task gets some processor attention. The system is operated in a round-robin fashion, where attention is returned to the first task after all the other tasks have been given a 'time slice'. It is more efficient than would appear at first sight, because some tasks may not need very much attention. One task, for example, might be waiting for a **peripheral** device to be free, and would thus be held in a **queue**, and its 'time slice' would be passed to the next **task**.

Token To avoid **collisions**, as can happen on **Ethernet networks**, an *electronic token is needed before any transmission of information can take place*. Only the machine with the electronic token may use the network, and other machines wishing to transmit information need to grab the token to be able to do this. The token is passed from one machine to the next so that all machines eventually get a turn. If a machine does not require the token it is immediately passed on to the next machine.

Token ring This is a **baseband network** based on sharing a **token**, and is *one method of implementing a* **Local Area Network**. A ring-shaped network (wired up in the form of a ring) in which a token (an electronic one) is grabbed before transmission of information can take place. Unlike **Ethernet**, this system ensures that *no* **collisions** can occur.

Top-down analysis This is a technique for splitting up a problem into sub-problems, which are then further split up into other sub-problems, possibly helped by making use of a **hierarchical diagram**.

Top-down design This is a design method where a *problem is split up into sub problems,* and, if necessary, *each sub problem is split up into further sub problems.* The top down design method can be conveniently expressed as a **hierarchical diagram**, because the highest level is at the top, and the lowest level of detail is at the bottom. *It is useful to do this because it allows teams of people to work on separate parts of a project.* Each part of the project can be tested independently making use of **unit testing**, before being integrated into the rest of the system and tested by using **integration testing**.

Top-level domain The *top-level* **Internet domains** are the '.com', '.uk' or '.org' etc. categories, which identify the type of organisation or the geographical location to which a particular domain belongs. For example '.edu' is an American academic organisation, '.ac.uk' is a British university or college that awards degrees, and '.fr' shows that a site is located in France. The '.com' is usually the most prestigious top-level domain to have, but the majority of sensible combinations of '.com' have already been taken.

Touch screen This is a **VDU** with *added sensors* (usually a criss-cross of infra-red beams) which *enables computer* **users** *to choose functions on the screen by touching the screen with their finger or other object.* It is useful in situations where it would be unrealistic to have a **mouse**. 'Machines in shopping malls', 'teller machines', 'photocopiers' and 'machines used with no supervision in public places' are good examples of this.

Touchpad This is *a surface which is used to control the cursor in a* **GUI** *environment.* It is popular on portable computers. **Users** can move their finger over the touchpad and this causes the **pointer** to move in sympathy with the movements of the finger on the pad. It is also possible to buy touchpads for use on conventional desktop **PCs**.

Trace A program trace is used to go through the *execution of a program* '**statement** *by statement' with the aim of trying to locate an error in the* **program**. A variety of help exists within some **program editors** that enable a trace to be done more effectively. This includes *single stepping* (executing one line at a time), *highlighting the line of code that is currently being executed,* and *producing a list of the state of the* **variables** at any moment in time. Similar **debugging** can also be accomplished manually by writing down the variables on a piece of paper, and then drawing up a table of what happens to the variables as the **program statements** are worked out in your head, but this is usually called a **dry run**.

Track ball *You can imagine this to be an upside-down* **mouse**. The finger or palm of the hand is used to move the **pointer** in a **GUI** environment by rolling the ball on top of this device. It is *ideal for use when there is little desk space*, or for use with a portable computer.

Training manual *These manuals are one of the ways in which* **training** *may be accomplished.* It would be usual to go through a training manual, practising with the system in front of you. There may be **CD-ROMs** which accompany this manual, providing examples of what to do and how to do it. There may also be banks of assessment and test questions to make sure that the **users** have understood the material in the manual. The training manual is *not necessarily* the same as **user documentation**, or a **user guide**, which is normally written for reference purposes.

Transaction *Transactions are simply another name for 'business deals' carried out in business each and every day.* This term is typically applied to processes like 'purchasing goods', 'joining a club', 'changing your doctor' or any other activity that is carried out by a particular business or other institution. At the end of the day, transactions might be stored in a special **transaction file** for **data processing** by the business or institution.

Transaction file A **data file**, usually containing **transactions**, like those that typically take place in a shop, for example. The list of items sold on a particular day would be a good example of this. See also **master file**.

Transducer This is the name given to devices which turn electrical energy into some other form of energy like sound, heat, light or motion, for example. When connected to a suitable computer, the computer may control a variety of systems from lights in a house to operating devices inside a car.

Transducer driver This is the name given to the **hardware** that drives **transducers** like 'motors', 'valves', or 'lights' etc. used when computers or other electronic devices are controlling external equipment.

Translation This is the act of *translating* **high-level languages** *into* **machine code**, using either an **interpreter** or a **compiler**, or *translating* **low-level languages** *into* machine code by *using an* **assembler**.

Transmission Control Protocol This is a common **protocol** used for transmission of data over **Internet** and **intranet** networks. It corresponds to the **transport layer** of the **ISO OSI model**.

Transport layer This is *layer four* of the **ISO OSI model**, and works with the **network layer** *to establish a reliable point-to-point connection between two hosts.* It does this by utilising error recovery methods, and establishes that the **data** is assembled correctly. The transport layer makes sure that **packets** are presented to the host in the right order, because they have been transmitted using a **virtual circuit**. The transport layer can also determine the most cost-effective route for transmission of the data, given the quality of service that is required (video, voice, computer data etc.). The transport layer links the **network layer** to the **session layer**.

Traversal This is a method of traversing (*going round*) **tree data structures** *visiting* **nodes** *as you make your way through the* **data structure**. There are three methods of traversal, namely **pre-order traversal**, **in-order traversal** and **post-order traversal**.

Tree structure A **data structure** in which the top level is known as the **root node**. *A tree structure can only have one root.* Most trees comprise different levels, and the entries at each level (including the root) are known as **nodes**. Just like a family tree, you can have **parent nodes**, **child nodes**, **brother nodes** and **sister nodes**. The nodes at the bottom of the tree are known as **terminal nodes** or **leaf nodes**. A tree structure mirrors many **hierarchical data structures** in real life, and is, therefore, very useful in computer science. A tree structure is usually implemented by using **pointers**.

Tree topology In **network topology**, a system where all the computers are connected to one or more **hubs**. *As hubs can be connected to other hubs, the system forms what looks like a tree.* The tree topology is the most common in the construction of **LAN**s using the popular **Ethernet** system. If just one hub is used, then the topology is sometimes referred to as a **star topology**.

Twisted pair *Cables, ideally suited to the transmission of* **data**, *are twisted together in pairs to help prevent electromagnetic interference.* Sometimes extra shielding is used in addition to the twisting to cut down interference even further. Cables like this are typically used on **Ethernet** networks. See also **CAT standard**.

Two-way linked list A **linked list data structure** with forward and backward **pointers**.

Two's complement A system of representing both positive and negative **binary** numbers. The system works in a way similar to a 'binary tape counter' where 000 would represent zero, and 001 would represent 1. However, wind 000 back one notch and you get 111, which represents −1. When two's complement notation is used the **most significant bit** represents the sign bit, which is 0 for positive numbers and 1 for negative numbers. This term should be compared with **sign and magnitude**. *It is vital that the 'exact number of bits' are specified when using this method or the wrong answers could be obtained.*

UML See **Unified Modelling Language**.

Unconditional jump *This is a term normally associated with* **assembly language** *programming.* Control is usually passed to another part of the program *unconditionally*. It is the same as the 'goto' instruction used in some unstructured **high-level languages.**

Unicode A two-**byte** system for *storing characters that represents virtually all languages in the World, including far-eastern languages like Japanese and Chinese*. This should be compared with **ASCII**, and **extended ASCII** which is suitable only for most western languages.

Unified Modelling Language This is *an industry standard way of producing diagrams* suitable for **systems analysis**, and is particularly suited to a structured **object-oriented analysis** approach. For the purposes of A2 computing, *you may use some of the* **UML** *diagrams to help undertake an object-oriented analysis in the* **design** *section of your module 6 project*. Using UML will help you to visualise, specify, build and document the features which you will use when analysing a project in which the chosen method of solution is an object-oriented programming language. *You need to do this if you have chosen to produce a solution using a language* like **C++**, **Java** or **VisualBasic.NET**. Specifically you will need to use **object analysis diagrams** (which are part of the UML) to produce **class diagrams**, which may be split up into **association diagrams**, **inheritance diagrams** and **aggregation diagrams**, You will also need to use class diagrams to show **class attributes** and **operations**. See also **object-oriented analysis** and **object analysis diagrams**.

Uniform Resource Locator *This is the address of a particular resource* on the **Internet**. An example of a URL is http://www.revisecomputing.com/project_work/index.htm. The first part *before the colon* specifies the **protocol** (like **http** or **ftp** etc.), the part after the '//' (but before the single '/') specifies the *name* of the **web server** which hosts the resource, and the part after the '/' specifies *the path to the location of this particular resource* on the server. In this case it is the index page for some project work. The '.com' part shows the **top-level domain** to which the site belongs. It is also possible to have parameters added to the URL, which act as **data** passed to **scripts** that interface with **search engines** and other **databases**. The **port** number (*not* shown here) can also be specified, but this is not frequently used, as a **default** of 80 is normally assumed for an http address.

Unit testing A small module of a project (*some piece of code or routine*) is tested *independently* before being joined with other units when **integration testing** is carried out. Testing may usually be carried out using **black box testing** or **white box testing** techniques. See also **integration testing**.

Universal Serial Bus *This is a very popular and fast* (**serial data communication**) *interface used to connect a huge variety of input and output devices* to the computer. Most devices like **printers**, **scanners**, **keyboards**, **mice** and **web cams** etc. can be connected via a USB port. UBS II is a faster version of the USB port.

Unix This is an **operating system** that is an alternative to Microsoft's Windows or Apple's Mac OS. It has been around for a considerable number of years and is well established and respected. The popular Linux is a Unix derivative.

URL See **Uniform Resource Locator**.

USB See **Universal Serial Bus**.

Usenet This is *world wide discussion forum based around* **Usenet newsgroups**. Much of Usenet is unregulated, and any person can post information on any topic.

User defined data type This is a **data type** in a **programming language** or **application** *which may be set up by the user*. In a programming language like **C++**, users may use the key word 'typedef' to define a range of data types in terms of other data types, or you might define your own data types in an **object-oriented database**, for example. This term should be compared with **built-in data type**.

User documentation This is the name given to the manuals that explain how to operate a system from the **users**' perspective. On a simple system this could include instructions regarding the **hardware** and **operating system** that are needed to run the system, how to install the **software** and how to use the software. Typically this manual might also contain some tutorials, a getting started section and more advanced techniques. On larger systems this documentation could run to thousands of pages.

User guide See **user documentation**.

User interface This is the interface between the *computer system* and the *people* who will use it. When designing a user interface, consideration must be given to how easy or effective the interface is to use, and whether it is appropriate for the intended purpose. E.g. a **concept keyboard** might be a more effective user interface for very young children compared with a conventional **keyboard**.

User manual This is an important part of your **A2 project**. *It is documentation separate from your main* *project, which is designed to help the* **user** *run the system on a day-to-day basis.* It is usually about 4 or 5 pages long, and can be in electronic form. It should help the user cope with likely errors that might occur with the system.

User name This is the same as the log on name, and enables people to be identified to either a local machine, or to **file servers** on an **intranet** or the **Internet**. The 'log on' or 'user name' is usually used in conjunction with a **password** for *authentication purposes.*

Users *The people who will be using the computer system.* The term is used extensively when referring to things like **user interface** and **GUI**. The term 'user' usually refers to *end users* rather than people, like **analysts** and **programmers** who are developing the system. However, the programmers would be 'end users' for companies like Microsoft, who sell development systems for **programming languages** like Visual Studio.NET, for example.

Users' schema This is the same as the *users' view* of a **database management system**. *It refers to the many different views that users may have of the same* **database** *via the* **DBMS**. Typically different views may be created by the front end to the database itself, via **programming languages**, or via **applications** such as **word processors** and **spreadsheets**. The **data control language** of the DBMS manages security, and ensures that users see only that data to which they are entitled.

Users' view A view of a **database management system** from the point of view of the end user.

Utility program A **program** that is specifically designed to *automate or accomplish common* **tasks** *when using the computer.* Typical examples would be programs to **defragment** the **hard disk**, copy **files** from one place to another, format a disk drive or perform diagnostic tasks on a malfunctioning computer.

Validation This is *one way of improving* **data integrity**. *Validation helps to ensure that data is sensible in the context in which it is being used.* It is unlikely, for example, that a person would be 200 years old, and validation checks on the inputted data would therefore ensure that a value like this does not get entered into the system. Range checks, checks on dates (e.g. 30th February should not get entered) and checks against a given list of valid data items would be just some of the methods used. *Don't confuse this term with* **verification**.

Value Added Network A Value Added Network is facilities provided by companies which offer services like 'mail forwarding', 'extra security provision' or 'access to specialist databases', for example. These companies would usually make a charge to a business for providing these services. Similar services could be set up by larger companies having their own infrastructure using **web servers**, database servers and mail servers for example, but these take a lot of expertise to set up and maintain, and smaller companies may prefer to use the facilities of a VAN provider. See **Value Added Network provider**.

Value Added Network provider This is a company that provides the services found on a **Value Added Network** or **VAN**. Typically these services may include 'electronic payments' or 'order management', for example.

VAN See **Value Added Network**.

Variable A *variable is a* **symbolic** *name used in a* **programming language** *for* **data** *that can take on a range of values.* Typical program variables might be 'x', 'Bank_Balance' or 'BookTitle'. Using a sensible name for a variable in a program makes it easier to read, and meaningful variable names should be used for good **structured programming** style. Most modern programming languages support long variable names, enabling the **programmer** to be able to use meaningful variable names to good effect.

Variable length record This may contain a variable number of fields or the fields may vary in length. All **records** within a **data file** may vary according to the **data** contained within the **fields** and **records**. This is a very efficient way for storing data, but it makes the **algorithms** for accessing the data more complex and time consuming, compared with a **fixed length record** structure.

Variable partitioning This is a term associated with **operating systems. Memory** *is allocated to programs and* **tasks** *in variable sized chunks.* This is harder to manage than **fixed partitioning**, but more efficient use is made of the memory, because the size allocated is more appropriate to the task being run, and the variable partitions can be dynamically allocated. Dynamic allocation (i.e. *allocation on the fly*) with variable partition sizes leads to the memory becoming **fragmented**, because new tasks are unlikely to require the same amount of memory as the memory vacated by the old tasks.

VBA See **Visual Basic for Applications**.

VBScript This is a *small program*, written in **Visual Basic** that runs inside a **web browser**, enabling the **user** to get increased functionality in terms of increased interaction. It performs a very similar job to **JavaScript**.

VDU See **Visual Display Unit**.

Vector A *number* stored in **memory** *used as a* **pointer** *to point to somewhere else.* A good example of its use is the **vectored interrupt** mechanism.

Vector-based graphic A **graphic**, made up from *mathematical relationships which are built up from vectors* (*straight lines*). Thus straight lines, curves (*many small straight lines*) and polygons (*whose sides are straight*) ensure that virtually any shape can be defined in either two or three dimensions. This type of graphic should be contrasted with **bit-mapped** or **pixel-based** graphics. Because of the mathematical relationships, the image can be magnified to extreme values without any loss of quality.

Vectored interrupt A **vector** *is used to point to a memory location where the actual* **interrupt handling routine** *resides.* The system is useful because it's easy to change where the **interrupt handler** is located in the computer's **memory map**. In this way *different* interrupt handlers can be added/modified and vectored into the system without changing anything other than the number (vector) which points to where the new **interrupt** is located.

Verification Verification means *checking something against another copy to see if it has been entered correctly*. E.g. when changing a **password**, you might be asked to verify the new password by typing it twice. If the two entries are identical, then the password has been verified as being correct, and the changes will take place. If the passwords are different, it did not pass the verification process, and you would be asked to type them in again. If important **data** is being entered into a computer, then two different people are sometimes used in the verification process, and the computer can be used as a check to see if the two **files** are identical. *Don't* confuse this term with **validation**.

Video capture card A **daughter board** plugged in to the main **motherboard** that handles video signals. If you wish to edit your own video material, or input images from a video camera into your computer, then a video card is normally needed to be able to do this. Most video cards come with a sophisticated range of **applications software** which allows you to edit the video clips you have taken previously, save them onto **disk** or to record them onto video tape.

Video editing *This is using a suitably high-powered computer, together with appropriate video-editing* **software** *to edit video footage*, usually created by video cameras. A very fast **processor**, a good **graphics card**, a **video card** and large **hard disk** capacity are needed to sensibly carry out video editing. The system would normally have the ability to write the video and sound tracks to **disk**, **CD** or **DVD** or to output a signal to VHS or SVHS tape.

Video input This is *getting a video signal into the computer*, either from a video camera or some other source like the output from a video cassette recorder. A **video card** is normally needed to do this.

Video-conferencing The use of computer **networks**, computers, video cameras, microphones, **interactive graphics tablets** and the like to make full two-way multimedia conferences possible. Special video-conferencing **software** enables the **users** to participate in talks and lectures by using this technology. A **LAN** or a **broadband connection** to a **WAN** would be needed to perform this effectively, preferably with **guaranteed bandwidth**.

Virtual circuit This is the name given to the *communication network that is used temporarily for the duration of a particular* **message** or **packet**. The next time the same computers communicate, the messages or packets might go via some completely different circuit, hence the name *virtual circuit*. Packets often arrive in the wrong order, but the **transport layer** of the **ISO OSI model** puts them back in the right order. See **message switching** and **packet switching**.

Virtual machine (1) This term is used to describe the concept that the **operating system** hides the complexities of the **hardware** from the user, providing an interface between the computer and the user.

Virtual machine (2) *This is the name given to the ability of* **multitasking operating systems** *to present different* **tasks** *to the* **user** *as though they are running on a different computer*. We could, for example, have a **word processor** running in one **window**, a **spreadsheet** running inside another, while a **DVD** movie is playing in a third. Each task appears to be running on a separate computer, and *this is like having three virtual machines*.

Virtual memory This is a technique of managing **files** or other **programs** too large to fit into the available **RAM**. Pages of memory are swapped between **RAM** and a **disk** drive, thus creating the illusion that you have more memory than you have physically got. However, if too much swapping takes place, this can slow down the computer considerably.

Virtual Private Network A Virtual Private Network is *an extension of a* **LAN**-*based* **intranet**, *making use of the* **Internet** *as the method of connection*. A VPN will make use of the **point to point tunnelling protocol** (**PPTP**). It enables **users** to have access to the facilities of their **LAN** from anywhere in the World. It keeps the LAN private by using strict access controls such as **passwords** and **strong encryption**.

Virtual reality helmets *This is a helmet (hat), worn by the user of a virtual reality system*. Images are projected inside the helmet so that the user thinks he or she is completely immersed inside a virtual computer world. As long as the images presented to the user's eyes cover a wide enough angle, the brain is convinced that the body is totally immersed inside the virtual world. It is this technique which makes flight simulators so successful.

Virtual reality input This is *a means of data input using equipment such as* **data gloves** *in combination with* **virtual reality helmets** and other equipment such as *whole body suits*.

Virus A computer **program** that is designed to cause annoying or catastrophic problems with the operation of a computer system. It is called a virus because it *infects the computer* and then *propagates* or *replicates* itself by using shared media such as **disks** and the **Internet** to infect other computers.

Virus checking Making use of **anti-virus software** to check to see if any viruses are likely to be present on a computer system. The virus check software will usually isolate or delete any viruses form the system.

Visual Basic *Microsoft's visual programming environment for* **BASIC**. It enables programmers to create **multitasking programs** in a drag-and-drop environment. This version of BASIC bears little resemblance to the earlier versions of **BASIC**, and the latest versions of **Visual Basic.NET** are fully **object oriented** and form part of the Visual Studio suite.

Visual Basic for Applications This is the **macro** language used for the Microsoft Office suite of programs. It is a subset of the **Visual Basic** language. It is used to extend the functionality of the office **applications**, by using macros either recorded by or written by the **user**, or derived from some **third party** source.

Visual Basic.NET A fully **object-oriented** version of Microsoft's **Visual Basic**. The methods needed to program in this language are significantly different from using previous versions of Visual Basic. The latest version of Visual Basic (the non object oriented version) will therefore be used for some considerable period of time, until most people are happy using the more complex **object-oriented programming** environment.

Visual Display Unit An *alternative name* for a computer **monitor** or a computer screen.

Volatile A term applied to semiconductor memory like **RAM**, which means that the contents (**data**) are lost when power is removed from the system. **Secondary storage** like **disks** should be used if the data is needed on a permanent basis.

Volumetrics This is *a study of how the sheer magnitude of a* **task** *might affect the way in which the* *system is implemented.* A print run of 1,000,000 copies per day, for example, would be treated very differently indeed from a print run of a few hundred copies per day, even though the same material is being printed.

VPN See **Virtual Private Network**.

WAN See **Wide Area Network**.

WAP See **Wireless Application Protocol**.

Weak encryption The number of **bits** used in the cryptographic key is such that the message can be deciphered *if you have enough supercomputing power*. Typically the amount of computing power found in a government research institution, where **supercomputers** could be used to do the number crunching. This term should be compared with **strong encryption**.

Web See **world wide web**.

Web address This is the address of a particular resource on the **Internet**. It is the same as a **URL**.

Web browser The **software** that displays **web pages** on a computer screen. The browser sends out a request for a web page and then displays the page when it is received. However, the functionality of even the simplest browsers go considerably beyond this, enabling the **user** to store frequently-used pages or look at previous surfing history, for example. Common examples of web browsers are Microsoft's Internet Explorer and Netscape's Navigator.

Web cam A small digital camera which captures moving video images in real time and (with the appropriate **software**) can be used to stream images to a **web site** for transmission over the **Internet** so they can be viewed by others using an appropriate **browser**.

Web hosting This is the name given to the process of storing a **web site** on a **web server** so that it can be viewed on the **Internet**. The web site is usually uploaded to the host's server by means of the **ftp protocol**.

Web page This is a single **html** document or file containing things like 'text', 'images' and 'sound' etc. When a **browser** requests a resource, a single web page is displayed at a time.

Web server This is a computer, permanently connected to the **Internet** (or an **intranet**) running special **software** that enables requests for **web pages** from **users' browsers** to be processed. In response to a request it will send out the appropriate web page to be viewed on a user's **web browser**.

Web site A *single entity* containing **html web pages**. In addition it is also likely to contain **scripts**, **databases** and other resources. The web site is stored on an **http web server** which controls access to these resources on an **intranet** or the **Internet**. Each web site has a unique address (**URL**), making use of the **Domain Name System**.

Web site address See **URL**.

Web-based form A *form on which* **users** *can type information into a* **browser**. The information then gets processed by the **web server** to which the user is connected. It is usual to enter **data** which gets put into a **database** on the server. In this way goods can be ordered from a shop or rooms in a hotel may be reserved or booked.

What if scenario This is when a **program** (usually a **spreadsheet**) is used to model scenarios in which important conditions are allowed to change, to see what effect changing these conditions might have. After the spreadsheet has **recalculated** the changes, it presents the new data on which the **user** can base a decision. A typical example might be a queuing simulation which simulates the number of checkouts needed in a supermarket. A client might be able to see *what* would happen to the length of the queues *if* the number of checkouts were changed. The decision to increase or decrease the number of checkouts, given a 'maximum queue length' and 'time to be served' could then be estimated. However, *the results are only as good as the mathematical model inside the spreadsheet.*

WHERE This is *a term associated with producing a query in a* **relational database**. The **key word** 'WHERE' is used to identify the **table** name from which **data** will be retrieved when using **SQL**.

White box testing White box testing involves *analysing* **program code** *to check the possible paths through the code*. This is usually accomplished by special **software**, but can be achieved by the use of **flowgraphs**. When individual paths have been identified, **black box testing** methods are used on each path.

Wide Area Network This is a **network** that makes use of external communication networks (e.g. telephone and satellite etc.) outside of the control of a **local area network** or **LAN**. Large numbers of resources like **servers, node computers** (**routers** and **gateways**) are needed to route the computer data around the system. The **Internet** is the biggest example of a **WAN**.

Wideband ATM A *faster version of* **Asynchronous Transmission Mode**, giving a **bandwidth** of just under 1 gigabyte.

WIMP **Windows**, **Icons**, **Menus** and **Pointers** form what's called the WIMP interface. This is an example of a **GUI**.

Windows (1) The name given to rectangular areas on the computer screen which act as a **virtual machine**. They usually have a 'title bar', 'scroll bars', and 'icons' to maximise, minimise and close the area. A window forms the basis of all **GUI operating systems**.

Windows (2) The name Microsoft has given to its popular range of **GUI operating systems**. Typical examples are the professional versions like Windows NT, Windows 2000 and Windows XP professional. Together with the home versions like Windows 98, Windows ME and Windows XP, these form the most popular operating systems on modern **PCs**.

Wireless Application Protocol This is a **protocol** *for enabling devices like portable computers,* **PDAs**, *mobile phones and the like to communicate with the* **Internet**. You have to have a special account with an **ISP** which provides the WAP enabled services. WAP is able to be used on a variety of wireless networks including mobile phone networks, pagers and some two-way radios.

Wireless Ethernet This is wireless-based **Ethernet** network technology. An Ethernet network may be set up without using wires because the **NIC** on the computers and the **hubs** etc. all have wireless connections (radio transmitters and receivers). The speed of operation is about 54 Mbit/sec, and is thus not as fast as most cable-based Ethernet networks. Nevertheless, it is very easy to set up and install, and allows people to roam around a site with a portable computer, while being connected to the Ethernet network without using wires. The range from the portable to the receiver on the network depends on the terrain and the type of wireless system being used. Extra security precautions like **firewalls** are essential because **hackers** using radio-based portables could attempt to hack into the network from outside the site.

Word A fundamental unit of storage on a particular **machine**, which usually relates to the *number of* **bits** *that can be processed at any one moment in time.* A word might be expressed in terms of the number of bits or **bytes**. We can thus have a two-byte word, or a **supercomputer** might have a 128-bit word, for example.

Word processor An **application package** *specifically designed for the sophisticated creation of text-based documents, in which most aspects of the text and layout may be changed very easily*. Most modern word processors also allow for the creation of simple pictures. A word processor should be compared with a **desktop publishing** package, and some very advanced word processors are as good as some elementary desktop publishing systems for the creation of complex documents. A good example of a word processor is Microsoft's Word.

Workstation (1) *The name given to a computer connected to a* **network**.

Workstation (2) *The name given to a powerful computer which can handle intensive processor and memory hungry applications like top-end* **CAD** packages, capable of rendering photo-realistic graphics in a sensible period of time. Ordinary PCs would take many hours or days to achieve these rendered results, although the latest 64-bit processors are getting close to doing a reasonable job.

World wide web *The system set up for linking billions of documents that are available on the* **Internet**. **Users** with a suitably equipped **web browser** may type in the **web address** of the **web site** of interest, and get the appropriate page downloaded from the **web server** and displayed on their screen. All computer-generated data like sound, video, text and pictures etc. can be displayed. *Don't* confuse the term **world wide web** with the term **Internet**.

WWW See **world wide web**.

WYSIWYG This means What You See Is What You Get. When using **word processors**, **desktop publishing** systems or high-end **web site** creation packages it's always easier to work by using a system that displays exactly what you will see in the final result (i.e. when the document is printed or the web page is published). If you are editing a web site using a simple **text editor**, for example, then all you would see is the **html code**, and not the WYSIWYG version.

XOR A **logical operation** which is virtually identical to the '**OR**' operation, *except for the condition in which all inputs are '1'; for an 'OR' operation the output would be '1' in this case, but the Xor eXcludes this condition and produces a '0' out instead.* This operation is usually available in both **high-level languages** and **low-level languages**.

Zip disk A proprietary brand of removable **hard drive** which can store either 100 Mbytes or 250 Mbytes depending on type. It is useful for small **backups** and **archives**.